TRANSMITTING CULTURE

EUROPEAN PERSPECTIVES

EUROPEAN PERSPECTIVES

A Series in Social Thought and Cultural Criticism

Lawrence D. Kritzman, Editor

European Perspectives presents outstanding books by leading European thinkers. With both classic and contemporary works, the series aims to shape the major intellectual controversies of our day and to facilitate the tasks of historical understanding.

For a complete list of books in the series, see page 156.

Transmitting Culture

Régis Debray

Translated by Eric Rauth

COLUMBIA UNIVERSITY PRESS   NEW YORK

Columbia University Press
Publishers Since 1893
New York   Chichester, West Sussex

Copyright © 1997 Editions Odile Jacob,
Translation copyright © 2000 Columbia University Press
All rights reserved

Library of Congress Cataloging-in-Publication Data
Debray, Régis.
[Transmettre. English]
Transmitting culture / Régis Debray ; translated by Eric Rauth.
p. cm. — (European perspectives)
Translation of: Transmettre.
Includes bibliographical references and index.
ISBN 0–231–11344–7 (cloth : alk. paper)
1. Knowledge, Sociology of. 2. Social values.
3. Socialization. 4. Culture diffusion.
I. Title II. Series
HM651.D4313 2000
306.4'2—dc21   99–087716

Printed in the United States of America
Designed by Audrey Smith

c 10 9 8 7 6 5 4 3 2 1

CONTENTS

Contents

PREFACE

Human beings have always transmitted their beliefs, values, and doctrines from place to place, generation to generation. How, by what strategies, and under what constraints do they persist in doing this? What essentials does this deceptively innocent transaction disguise? These are the questions I wish to reassess and work through afresh in this book.

Matters such as these have known a pitiless translation into actions and things on the proving ground of historical fact, leading one to wonder why, for example, certain ideas and not others become material forces. From what causes does their influence derive, and does it properly belong to them? How can one explain the fact that certain words, at certain moments, can have earth-shattering effects? Or that some have left their traces and traditions while others have not? Why should one promise-proposition of eternal salvation have transformed itself into the empire's state religion in preference to another? Why did a secular plan for regenerating humanity spread over a half-century to become, for a time, a planetary orthodoxy, when other ideologies of the same age and intellectual substance soon repaired to the libraries? Why, to put it clearly, did Jesus finally take hold among masses of people, *urbi et orbi*, rather than Mani the Mesopotamian or the eastern god Mithra? Why did Karl Marx leave his mark of blood and iron on the century, and not, say, Pierre Proudhon or Auguste Comte? And from these singular cases, these circumstantial thus irreducible bifurcations, can one infer certain laws of general import concerning the powers of thought and the transformational dynamic of ideas?

Transmitting meanings in culture, to come back to the outline of a knowable subject, still seems at this time to be a theme whose implications have not yet been explored and pinned down. It floats alongside, or outside, the routines of several disciplines of study that by now benefit from well-honed arguments and premises, such as sociology, the history of thought, genetics, and epidemiology. When it comes to the mediological question of *how meanings are materially transmitted*, however, these disparate fields show no congruence of focus. My intention is to contribute to finding a firm and proprietary foundation for a mediology, to make it an object of thought (though not of science, a claim as naive as it is hubristic).

To propose upgrading a self-evident fact—namely, that cultural meanings are transmitted—into a problem, to construct an object of substance out of scraps, meant opening up a work site for criticism with its own demarcations. It meant asking that an original sector of research be identified and dedicated to the facts of cultural transmission as an object of study in its own right. It then seemed useful to affix a sign that identified the materials on this construction site. "Mediology" seemed to encompass them well enough as labels go. Its authorship, exact date of conception, and virtues and vices as a tag, a label, matter little. There is no patent on the term.

It is not as if coining a word were all that was needed to define a concept. As if knowledge were better served by an arbitrarily imposed edict than by finely shaded and modest analysis. As if we have not already suffered enough from the power game of neologism, from the pompous trappings of announced research projects, deferring to tomorrow the definitive explanation. As if a scrupulous inventory of innumerable empirical labors pertaining to the topic should prove any less sterile than one of those pretentious and turgid systems certain Anglo-Saxons like to impute to *l'esprit français*.

These are legitimate reservations and precautions. The throng of *-ologies* tossed in a rush into the bargain bin of innovation and lasting only as long as their authors do would be enough to justify them. But I will try here to show the component of prejudice in such suspicious reflexes, which a second look will perhaps mitigate. An attempt or a wager? The laws of intellectual competition being what they are, nobody is unaware of the artificial situation facing anyone intent on defining and projecting an as-yet-uncertain edge into a domain of reality. Such a field is unendowed with social and scientific legitimacy. If its author does not present forthwith his theoretical claims to existence and his method's cornerstones, he will be labeled as an artist or essayist: a chic eclectic, a playful banterer. If he endeavors to adduce his own monographs as part of the argument, to conceptualize however minimally his own work, he will err very probably through a vain formalism, aligning superficial analogies, uncontrolled metaphors, and hasty generalizations. For this, he will be described as pontificating and daydreaming. Thus it is without illusions that I undertake this task, fully conscious of the infinite spaces that separate me from the threshold of positivity and more so of scientificity but convinced, at this gestational stage, of the necessary passage from sampling instances to perceiving the whole.

Singleness of purpose has been one of my goals of inquiry. Whether focusing up to this point on the scribe and the history of intellectuals, on the contemporary state and its functioning, on the manufacture of images and their transformation, on the spectacle, on roadways or the nation, I believe I have worked my subject, on numerous occasions, in full view, using descriptive sketches. It is not my ambition now to go in for one of those exercises in prophetic generalizing, those apocalyptic homilies apparently called for by the millennium's end and its catastrophic stridencies. The objectivity employed here with regard to the concerns and targets of observation is demanded by any return to the basics of an approach, in order to think through its agenda and subject it to critical adjustment and emendation. The sole concern is to thicken the analysis of the real while reducing the multiplicity of its operative aspects to intelligible patterns. It is doubtless not the best painters who produce treatises of painting. Fortunately, the mediological field is common land. It is relatively open. And it counts in its ranks enough original and productive groundworkers that few should bear this book ill will for being a survey course given behind closed doors by a pedant.

ACKNOWLEDGMENTS

My gratitude goes to all the coorganizers of *Les Cahiers de médiologie*, whose friendly debates and discussion have sustained and enlivened this development of the question. Catherine Bertho-Lavenir, François Bernard Huyghe, Louise Merzeau, and Monique Sicard, in particular, readily shared their observations and critical comments. From within her own area of research, Nathalie Heinich provided gracious help with her expert sociological judgments. And I thank Bernard Stiegler not only for having led me to rediscover André Leroi-Gourhan's writings but for the guiding elucidations of his own work.

TRANSMITTING CULTURE

The Medium's Two Bodies

Tedious quarrels over semantics can often be avoided, and time gained, by securing argument to a few working definitions at the outset. I differentiate the material act of transmitting from communication, the latter term having by now lost some concreteness as the sanctified hallmark of language theoreticians and university programs or departments. To the degree that units of relatively stable meaning can be made fast from words of such voluminous carrying capacity and guaranteed currency, the semantics of *communication* do appear, in every detail, to be set squarely against the material objects and forces intelligible to mediological inquiry. Instead, *transmission* can serve as a regulatory and classificatory term in view of its tripartite signification: material, diachronic, and political.

THE MATERIAL DIMENSION

Commonly understood, "communicating" is simply making familiar, making known. Its bias of meaning links us immediately with the immaterial, with conventions and codes, with the more narrowly linguistic. One speaks, on the other hand, of "transmitting" physical property as well as ideas. Commercial bills, assets and real estate, a child's balloon can all be transmitted in the sense of handed over or down, as can orders and instructions or papal power. What is said of forms is also said of forces: in mechanics, the term *transmission* is applied to power and movement that are carried across—transmitted—by mechanical means, dynamically converted to different forms of motion.

This alloy of material agencies and human actors is well suited to the vast and bustling agitation of infinite motive forces that, in a succession of historical instances, characterizes what used to be called "an idea that stirs the masses." *Idea* connotes that convocation, mobilization, *jumble* of engines and persons, passwords and icons, vehicles, sacred rites and sites. To this day, for example, the gospel's message makes its appeal to followers via canticles and holy days, the church's swell of organ notes and glitter of gold, the colors of its stained glass and altarpieces, the perfumes of its incense, the soaring spires of its cathedral and shrines, the wafer's placement on the tongue and the foot's tread on the road to Calvary. These materializations and exertions, rather than individual or group exegesis of sacred texts, bodily *transmit* the holy Word. The same holds for civil religion. The idea of the nation is perpetuated by flags and solemn commemorations of the dead, by the entombment of soldiers and monuments to the fallen on the village square, by lists of their names on walls and plaques and pediments, by the domes of pantheons, and not merely by reading textbook summations or preambles of constitutions. Memory's reinforcements cannot be reduced to sayings and writings. The adventure of lived ideas is hurly-burly and kaleidoscopic.

No tradition has come about without being an invention or recirculation of expressive marks and gestures. No movement of ideas has occurred that did not imply the corresponding movement of human bodies, whether pilgrims, merchants, settlers, soldiers, or ambassadors. And no new dimension of subjectivity has formed without using new material objects (books or scrolls, hymns and emblems, insignia and monuments). The sites where associations are generated weld together the heaven and earth of faiths and doctrines by plotting the dizzying vertical of their sacred allusions along the horizontal axis of collective consolidations. As Christian or Jew or Arab, I affirm my ties to the community of fellow celebrants by traversing the space separating me from Santiago de Compostela, Jerusalem, or Mecca. A Marxist in the 1960s, I further my ideological adhesion with pilgrimages to Havana or Hanoi, just as, more prosaically, I might attend the Festival of Humanity sponsored by the French Communist daily newspaper. A committed neoliberal, I'm off to communion at Westminster or Wall Street because reading articles by Milton Friedman or works by Karl Popper hardly suffices. The chain of effects that transform mentalities mingles together elements both symbolic and economic, immaterial and concrete, such that a mediologist's interest will be repaid as much by the minutiae of foreign missionaries as by theologies, the Wall of Jerusalem as by the Kabbalah, humble modes of transport as by sublime myths of origin, the highways department as by schools of philosophical thought; by networks of transmission as much as by doctrines, and the material bases of inscriptions as much as by the etymologies of words. In short, the trivial, peripheral, or basely material incidentals of how any given message, doctrine, or idea is put across mean as much to the mediologist as (Plutarchian) "exemplary lives" or "great books." Far from inviting disciplinary confusion, this muddle of mediating agencies calls for theoretical clarification that must first demolish some arbitrary walls between established fields.

THE DIACHRONIC DIMENSION

If communication transports essentially through space, transmission essentially transports through time. Communication prompts an instantaneous response between parties, by synchronizing and connecting them like a thread: a communicative network runs its course between contemporaries (sender and receiver present to one another simultaneously at either end of the line). Transmission takes its course *through* time (diachronically), developing and changing as it goes. A thread *plus* a drama, it links the living to the dead, most often when the senders are physically absent. Whether configuring the present to a luminous past or to a salvific future, mythical or not, a transmission arranges the effective force of the actual with reference to the virtual. As far as communications are concerned, time is external to them in the sense of its being only their parameter (even though by overcoming distances, *tele*communications do have an effect necessarily on the amount of time by which delays and speeds are determined). But with transmission, time is appreciable internally. Communication excels by cutting short; transmission by prolonging, even if it must condense its ample forms of expression into the emblematic currencies of the motto, the logo, the apologue, the parable, and so on. Religion, art, ideology: these variegated categories of transmission all aim to thwart the ephemeral by the ploy of drawing out, particularly in the Western context, with its grand undertakings of constructions built to last.[1]

The two terms thus require a shift in scale and units of time: for the operation of communication, a calculation of days, minutes, and seconds; for transmission, decades if not centuries and millennia. We transmit meanings so that the things we live, believe, and think do not perish with *us* (as opposed to *me*). To accomplish this, we have license (depending on the historical period) to invent the means of oral epic poetry, with its rhythms and ritornellos conducive to memorization; or the arts of drawing or writing; or printing, audiocassettes, CD-ROMs, or the World Wide Web, as the search for target user audiences or technological developments dictates.

The content of the message is guided by the requisites of its deliverance, as is the organ by its function. Though measurably temporal, transmission does have a geography. Its advancement occupies space, but it conducts its crossings and bids for influence in order to make inroads toward permanence, to *make history* (the pervasive desire to pervade time by turning any means it can to account). While a communication society will value the disposable, mutable, and instantaneously accessible, the depth of time rounds out the things that are transmissible and gives them relief and dimension. In the one case, continuance is only an accident; in the other, it is crucial. The evanescence of a message will compromise an act of transmission, but it will not disqualify a communication. Within the nascent discipline of mediology one has the habit of distinguishing among messages according to their material natures as sounds, sights, written words, audiovisual sequences, and so on. From the vantage of cultural significance, however, the fact that a given sense perception is objectified and safeguarded in durable form matters more than the particular faculty in question (hearing, vision, etc.). The information's recovery and repetition counts for more than the channel carrying it or its specific material nature.

THE POLITICAL DIMENSION

Human beings *communicate*; more rarely do they *transmit* lasting meanings. Communication's horizon is individualistic. Its one-on-one matrix of sender to receiver has marked for a good while now the study of the more industrialized, general diffusion of messages (circulation, broadcasting, the wide dissemination of language and ideas) based on a one-to-all relation. (Widespread cultural diffusion by technological media really began with Gutenberg and not McLuhan and with the practice of engraving before that of photography.)

The contrast is thus stark, to my way of thinking, between the warmer and fuzzier notion of communication and the militant, suffering nature of the struggle to transmit. Here the communicational fiction of the lone individual producing and receiving meaning gives way to people establishing membership in a group (even if only one they seek to found) and to coded procedures signaling that group's distinction from others. There is a sense in which the natural environment *communicates* information about itself to me through visual, tactile, olfactory, and other senses. Even more can I say that animals give off or send out messages: the science of zoological semiotics makes them an object of study. But I cannot speak of animals, nor of my physical surroundings, as *transmitting* per se. *Everything* is a message, if you will—from natural to social stimuli or from signals to signs—but these messages do not necessarily constitute an inheritance. Legacies are never the effect of pure chance. Similarly, there are *communication* machines but not *transmission* machines. At most, one can define an act of transmitting as a *tele*communication in time, where the machine is a necessary but not sufficient interface and in which the network will always mean two things. For the pathway or channel linking senders and receivers can be reduced to neither a physical mechanism (sound waves or electric circuit) nor an industrial operating system (radio, television, computer) as it can be in the case of diffused mass information. The act of transmitting adds the series of steps in a kind of organizational flowchart to the mere materiality of the tool or system. The technical device is matched by a corporate agent. If raw life is perpetuated by instinct, the transmitted heritage cannot be effective without a project, a projection whose essence is not biological. Transmission is duty, mission, obligation: in a word, culture.

Communication and transmission must both contend with the problem of *noise*. Yet here, on top of the physical universe acting as backdrop, must be overlaid the social universe in all its adversity. A cost is borne by every communication because no message-producing condition or device can wrest the meaning of a signal from its ambient background noise without an expenditure of energy to neutralize the natural and accidental static that afflicts all signals. But putting across a symbolic, transmissive meaning must also deal, beyond the loudspeaker's metallic coughs and reverbs, with the splutters and crackle of one's adversaries and competitors. More than an incidental flawing of the system or unintended disorder, this latter form of noise arises from human conflict at the heart of the mediasphere's acoustic space of deliberation. As in the Darwinian biosphere, place is not available to all. This is what makes each transmission work itself out polemically, and it requires a strategic competency bent on striking up alliances, filtering out and excluding the extraneous, hierarchizing and co-opting, drawing boundaries, and so on. The process can be apprehended as a struggle for survival in the midst of a system of rival forces either canceling one another out by disqualification or swallowing each other up.

In the *social* arena, other things being equal, the act of communicating anything and everything is natural. Transmitting durable meanings, however, belongs to the *political* arena, as do all functions serving to transmute an undifferentiated mass into an organized whole. Through transmission, a collective organization is immunized against disorder and aggression. A protector of the coherence of an *us*, it ensures the group's survival by apportioning what individuals hold in common. What survives moreover does not fall under the class of the most basic biological group programming, such as the automatic processes of eating and reproducing, but rather under all things having to do with the collective personality granted the group by its own history. If communication takes place between persons, transmission uses collegial methods and collective settings, frameworks, and management. It is one of the stakes of civilization. It brings about unification into corporate entities such as professional guilds, mystical corpuses, or the teaching corps of sorcerers, bards, elders, Greek epic singers, clerics, pilots, instructors, catechists, and so on. By this means the corpus of knowledge, values, and know-how is brought out of yesterday into the present, stabilizing group identity via multiple two-way journeys (made by each member of a confraternity, an academy, a church, a craft guild, a school, a party, a nation, etc.). They are the group's master thread, the safeguard at the ramparts and parapet, the guardrail.

The indispensableness of this symbolic function is matched by the discretely grave aura that hovers over the word *transmission*. Essences are made and remade through transmission; the torch thrown to each new generation, which must hold it high, says the common wisdom. One can communicate with the first passerby, but such things as the sacred flame, capital (and the sinfulness of human nature), the spirit of one's homeland (down to the very taste of its baked bread), all these are *transmissible*. Transmissible, too, are great secret stories or practices: family secrets, state secrets, secrets of the heart; arcana of the Book, of calculating longitude and making metals; professional secrets, party secrets, secrets of the gods and nature. Preserving all these gives a community its reasons for being and hoping. One has no right to forget or keep them to oneself, and to squander them would be to forfeit what must be held dearest. They are not something hastily communicated sub rosa but rather more as mysteries into which one is by degrees initiated, heart and soul. Journalists communicate; professors transmit. (The difference is that between news and knowledge.) Notaries arrange for inheritances, a priest enshrines a tradition (laws versus rites). Communication needs only interest and curiosity. Proper transmission necessitates transformation if not conversion. When fear and trembling ensue, the result is the only criterion. Thus is the process of education, for example, inconceivable without its regulations, examinations, or competitions for prizes.

THE MECHANICS OF TRANSMISSION

The prefix *trans-*: it comes down most decisively to this particle that encapsulates the marching past, burden, and adventure of so many mediations. And yet what the term alludes to could not be more prosaic. *Le Petit Robert* gives the following definition for *transmission*:

> trans-mis-sion *n.* [L. *transmission-*, *transmissio*, fr. *transmissus*, pp. of *transmittere* to transmit fr. *trans-* across, over + *mittere* to send] [1765, used to speak of electronic signals. 1869, telegraphic signals.] Transference of a physical phenomenon or of its effects when this transference implies one or several intermediate factors capable of affecting the phenomenon.

There can be no transmission of movement, in the mechanical sense, without machine parts that produce it (camshaft, universal joint, drive wheel, drive belt). And in medical parlance, no transmission of disease, epidemiologically speaking, can occur without a site for the pathogen and an infectious agent. Communications can be of an immediate, direct, and joyously transitive nature. Transmission, on the other hand, imposes itself on us by its character as process or mediation, something that dispels all illusion of immediacy. Mediology is devoted to medium and median bodies, to everything that acts as milieu or middle ground in the black box of meaning's production, between an input and an output. A milieu: it is indeed because there is refraction that there is degradation. The *transmission coefficient* (or ratio between the intensity of influential radiance after its passage through a given milieu and its initial intensity) also affects the emission of immaterial abstractions.

To sum up, if it is true that one cannot separate completely, in vivo, the range of phenomena encompassed by *communication* and *transmission*, one must guard against mixing them together. In vitro, we can do this by subordinating the first, more modern notion to the older one, which seems to me at once more holistic and more rigorous. A process of transmission necessarily includes acts of communication. The converse of this may not occur; here, the whole will have primacy over the part. To reflect on the nature of transmission illuminates communication, but the reverse does not hold true. It is highly unlikely that a communications major or the holder of an advanced degree in communications arts will have studied the origins and formation of the West's most popular religion. But anyone curious enough to adopt a mediological approach and follow the propagation of the "true faith" across its first few centuries will have also gleaned in passing some insight into information societies in the year 2000.[2] (Turning one's back on a problem is often the best way to pose it the most aptly.)

Not a single historical reconstruction (however partial) of communitarian crystallizations—be they far back in time or closer to us, perennial or fleeting, revealed religions or rational utopias, or two movements that most interest me: primitive Christianity and proletarian socialism—can properly fit under the purview of communication studies/computer science. Faith in the living Jesus was no more propagated by the newspaper than was Marxism over the telegraph wires. Access to these hotbeds of meaning was not a simple matter of communicative instantaneousness or spontaneity. Their complex means of constituting themselves slowly and symbolically exceed in every detail and import what we today call means of communication. Mediation does not reduce to media. Shelving a more philosophically informed mediology in the media studies section would be as sagacious as considering the study of the unconscious a part of the sciences of the occult. It has been known to happen. And this blunder proves unfortunate.

CIRCUMSCRIBING A DISCIPLINE

Transmission it shall be. But of what, exactly? Once we set apart a new field of study, it remains to explore fully the object. How to avoid the pitfalls of seeing things everywhere transmitted, from the AIDS virus to property holdings to titles of nobility to a privilege to bad character? The human sciences already label *reproduction* the past's continuance into the present.[3] It should be said I have in mind neither (1) the properly biological reproduction of a group nor (2) a group's social reproduction in a global sense, even if the latter can be likened to transmitting a cultural or symbolic capital. The separation of fields, necessary to scientific progress, always has something arbitrary about it. Codes' transmission has no autonomous and pure existence, which is also why the semiologists' insistence on the arbitrary nature of the sign hardly suffices as a basis on which to analyze the workings of society or technology. Even if the influence one exerts can never be reduced to a power one imposes, and even if symbolic violence is by definition differentiated from physical coercion—the first presumably beginning where the second ends—the action of one will or mind on another is indistinguishable from the institutional or informal positions of power held by them. Leader and foot soldier, guru and follower, witch doctor and patient, father and son, president and citizen, boss and employee, general and private: these oppositions are realities, not arbitrarily binary. Study of transmission can obviously not exclude all that occurs among members of a family or at school, in the neighborhood or village (a father, for instance, transmits certain norms and values to his children without even saying a word, as does membership in a union). But at this early stage I would rather concentrate on how explicit symbolic systems are perpetuated: on religions, ideologies, doctrines, and artistic productions. I do not ask how the social world reproduces its constitutive structures such as the state, the family, property, social classes, and the like, nor how the sociocultural predispositions of agents in that world (wage earners, teachers, supervisors, spouses, bureaucrats, etc.) are reproduced from generation to generation, but rather, how is it that, two thousand years after Jesus, there still subsists something like Christianity in the Western world; or, more than a century after Marx and Darwin, something like Marxism and Darwinism; or, more than fifteen years following Lacan's death, Lacanian analysis; and so on. What are the pathways followed by the relay race of human thought (a subject overflowing the mere transactions of language)? Where are the sites at which, somewhere between myths and figuration, a new or different meaning is added to something that had possessed none, or another, before?

This said, I do not intend to dwell in that innocent empyrean of popular zeitgeist phantasms, that undifferentiated haunt of the gods and spectral collective representations. This is because these productions of consciousness—religions, doctrines, ideologies, disciplines—impinged decisively on the course of material things. They had direct influence on organized bodies and human bodies, modifying how they functioned politically, economically, and militarily, rather than working only in peoples' dreams and minds. The administration of signs and images has effects and stakes that are tangible, constraining, and at times violent. Neutral things mobilize energies, inert things act on us, and the word giveth life. No doctor remains unaware of the placebo effect, which pharmaceutical labs now isolate and measure. A host of today's historians have, I dare say, fully caught up with the pharmacists. Their fertile researches encourage a certain formal leap toward a discipline whose object is the relations between the superior social functions of art, religion, and ideology and the sociotechnical structures of transmission, in other words, ipso facto, *the ways and means of cultural symbols' efficacy.* Such a methodical undertaking would not lack import for those present sciences of the collective that, when they turn to the still mysterious effects of peoples' beliefs, resort more often than not to metaphor over explanatory analysis.

ORGANIZED MATTER AND MATERIALIZED ORGANIZATION

Consider from the outset an intelligible, deliberately schoolish model (only by pressing the limit cases, however reductive, do we release an explanatory force that makes it easier to grasp yesterday's and today's confusion of certain issues). The development of tool-using hominids from evolutionary lines leading back to common ancestors of man and apes, on the grand scale of paleontology, was driven by countless functional collaborations between inert matter and biological living matter. So too does the acculturation of a distinct group, on the historical scale, couple *communication* with *community.* It is the wedding of the technological factor to the institutional factor, by and within the process of social incorporation, that sheds light on the paradoxical currentness of the past. It also helps explain the enigma of human history as a succession without exteriority.

What poet does not expect his utterance to survive its initial inspiration? Where is the striker of meaning's sparks who does not wish to set fire to the plain? Indeed in order to bring off transmission across time, to *perpetuate* meaning, in my capacity as emitting Everyman I must both render messages material and convince others to form into a group. Only working on dual fronts to create what will be memorable by shaping those devoted to it can elaborate the milieu for transmission. The memorable can be put across by transforming what has perished into monuments (because physical matter preserves the traces of what is absent). Those who do the remembering, the *mémorants,* or remembrancers, constitute collective official channels of re-creation (because only the living can stir the embers of meaning that slumber in traces of the past). Together, matter and members make up Bergson's so-called two sources of morality and religion, the cold and the hot: a mortal, or objective, memory and a living, or innovative, memory. They bind together indissolubly, in the manner of a passive *cultura culturata* and an active *cultura culturans* or, to use the terms of medieval scholasticism, material cause and efficient cause. Communication is the message's sine qua non, while the com-

munity of messengers is that *by* which the choice of an inheritance is possible. The message that does not find an institutional housing will go up in
smoke or be drained off as so much background noise by the ambient environment of cultural life. Perpetuating meaning assigns an institution the dual
mission of archival and pedagogical conservation. No prophetic or charis-
matic improvisations can substitute for it, and it exceeds all individual capac-
ities. The institution acts as a kind of registry or patent office, but rather than
passively conserving its charges, it is never done sifting, revising, censuring,
interpreting, and peddling them. It also authorizes others in turn to pass on
its achievements or even to deflect and divert them. The church through its
preaching, the university through its teaching, the Freudian brotherhood
through its psychoanalyzing are all forms for conferring pertinent qualifica-
tions in their respective competencies. Their task takes on a dynamism when
it is oriented outward, yet it implies a certain inertia on the inside.

We can rough-hew a further elaboration. The agencies of cultural
expression belong to one of two orders: inorganic and organic. Medieval
cosmologists divided up extant beings, on the one hand, into organized
beings (the object of the sciences of life) and, on the other, inanimate things
(objects of the physical sciences). The operation of culture invents and
mobilizes a third and fourth category of existents of which our knowledge,
in contrast to the preceding antitheticals, is still quite imperfect and will no
doubt occupy the centuries to come: the categories of organized matter and
materialized organization.

Man-locomotive contrasts with the errant animal in his aptitude for making movement coagulate into a solid structure (Georg Simmel). Even so, the
organized inorganic is not to be attributed solely to the human species.
Animals do after all produce works of art (or industriousness?) even if they do
not labor from a plan. Swallows construct their nests, bees their hives, beavers
their dams, and moles their burrows. The same holds for materialized organizations inasmuch as, broadly speaking, we can speak of societies of termites,
the organized activity of ants, and the like. Peculiar to humanity is its particular combinations for materializing organization and organizing matter.

A labor of transmission can be broken into its two corporatist components: its constituent body of members or service staff (a corps in the sense
of diplomatic corps or teaching corps) and its material embodiment (its
body in the sense of "falling bodies" in physics). We see the complexity of a
process that summons the mythological talents of the artisan and the legis-
lator, the machine maker and the lawgiver, Daedalus and Lycurgus. At the
material level, to transmit is to inform the inorganic by manufacturing con-

sultable stores of externalized memory through available technologies for inscribing, conserving, inventorying, and distributing the recorded traces of cultural expression. At the institutional level, transmission means structuring the social locus in the guise of collective organized units, devices for filtering out mere noise, and totalities that endure and transcend their members of the moment and reproduce themselves over time under certain conditions, all at high costs (such as those nonbiological "living" beings: a school of thought, a religious order, a church, a party, or an institution of learning). What would happen without such materialized organization, this pocket of antientropy, this enclave of ordered activity hewn out of the larger amorphous disorder? Such a micromilieu is constituted only at considerable effort, as it is a quasi-substantial form set off from a more or less amorphous environment. Simply translating organized matter across homogeneous space and time directly and uncomplicatedly—say, in the way one translates a triangle in mathematics or, in physics, the way a translated moving body has all its points in motion at any instant going at the same velocity and direction, as opposed to those of a rotating body—would merely *transfer* or *displace* it. It would not address all those conditions and changing contexts whose resistance both impedes and allows organized matter to be put across. Just translating organized matter would subject it maximally to those very conditions and contexts—to static, loss of signal, fossilization, repetition, and extinction—for forging a chain of meaning to impede its dissolution obliges one to remake its living links incessantly, like living stones in the edifice of the Gospels. All in all, *just as there can be no cultural transmission without technological means, so is there no purely technological transmission.*

Among the varieties of organized materials required to materialize organizations must be included a proper orchestration of all the instruments of communication. One can distinguish between (a) the *semiotic mode* (the type of sign used, be it textual, imagistic, or audible); (b) *the form of its distribution, broadcasting, or channeling* (linear, radial, interconnected, or networked); (c) *its material base* (stone, wood, papyrus, paper, or waves); and (d) *the means of transportation* (of people and messages, via roads, vehicles, infrastructures, and larger systems and industries). Rendering the message material, let us not forget, means not only drawing (or keying) signs but also opening ways for them to reach others. Among organized matter's artifacts you will find, according to the given mediasphere, ink and copper plates as well as communications satellites; parchment, calamus reeds, and styluses for writing, as well as PCs and typewriters; and horses' saddles, along with automobiles and telegraphs.

Under materialized organization, or institutions, you can lay out communitarian arrangements, that is, all those diverse forms of group cohesion
that bring together the human agents of a given transmission or, more
exactly, those forms *imposed on* such agents by the material nature of whatever coded signs and devices they are using (a function of the regnant stage
of semiotic development). Your list will include chains of command, per-
sonnel, and bureaucracies; priests, rabbis, mullahs, and professors; salons
and plebeian tribunes; steering committees and ancient Roman and
Catholic curias and consistories; institutes, academies, and *collèges*; chief
curators and revolutionary chieftains. Take for example the tradition and
institution of cinematic image making. Cinema is the sum of film clubs and
celluloid. Especially in the French context, it groups together organizational methods that originated from the confluence of activist Catholicism and
political progressivism—the review, the club, the festival, and journalistic
criticism—together with evolving representational technologies, such as
projectors, cameras and shooting angles, soundtracks, screening procedures, and so on.

In sum, the art of transmission, or making culture, consists of adding a
strategy to a logistics, a praxis to a techne, or establishing an institutional
home and engineering a lexicon of signs and symbols. What persists over
time is the art of composition; the proportion of elements varies.

As a general rule, the stronger the innovatory force of a given symbolic
message (i.e., the greater its nonconformity with the norms of its milieu),
the sturdier must be its transmission's organizational armature, because it
will become all the more arduous to clear ways through hostile surroundings. For its part, the transmissive relay will see to it that a certain necessary
level of redundance is sustained for the sake of a proper hearing. Because an
excess of originality affects reception adversely, one must know how to use
signs that are dispensable—or already familiar to the ambient milieu—to be
understood. In the science of perfumes, a nondiluted fragrance can become
toxic or noxious (the Mallarmean enigma); the mediologist's art avoids this
pitfall, pouring the banal into the original, as water stretches wine.

Historians contend there could have been no Roman Empire (materialized organization) in the absence of roads (organized matter); geographers,
no roads in the absence of empire. What was the ultimate causal operative in
these historical efforts to domesticate space and time? Doubtless it was the
collectively authorized individual authority that accumulated capital and
commanded construction (the project manager-state, in the case of the road
system). The *who* as subject of the predicate of transmission is a motive force

vis-à-vis its *what*. In the Marxist schema of determinations, organized matter is considered *instrumental* in producing both (1) a projected meaning, i.e., organized matter's mode of production, the macrosystem of transmission currently in force (itself the hybrid of different superimposed technological periods); and (2) the productive force of that projected meaning, i.e., the collectivity that variously takes in, takes down, and puts out cultural meanings. In these orderings of the world, material organizations put things in motion; in the example, the Roman Empire clears land to lay roads allowing its legions to go forth and return more easily, its food supplies to be absorbed, its hegemony to be carried on. All of which supposes, among other things, the organized and appropriative network of routes for sending communiqués, receiving reports, and transporting troops that subsequently spread Christianity through the channels already put in place under the old empire, lending the new culture the old's imprimatur.

A necessary but not sufficient causality, then, the concept of instrumentation can propose but not dispose. Precisely for this reason, no single cultural form is pregiven in the material technical system that makes it possible. *Verbi gracia*—thanks to the Word—the system of alphabetic writing did indeed enable the ancient Greek city to become a meeting ground for those who could read to be exposed to public decision making and debate. But, by the same token, this publicness required the institutional machinery of politics in order to promote graphic reason to its new standing. Mediation is a zigzag.

Likewise, the institution or tradition of painting would not have come about as art without the art gallery, the site of its appreciation and sale, with all the attendant regulated capitalization of daubed canvases this implies. Yet there could never have been a modern museum without first a politically motivated creation of the national patrimony, a matter of institutional authority. Likewise, no literature without a library; in France, no *royal* library without a Charles V to promote it or *national* one without the Revolution's Jacobin phase.[4] No edification without the struggle to build the edifice. In other words, no historical record of memory records itself. Downstream, its trace has the virtue, or vice, of effacing the collective trace leaver upstream. Roman roads outlive the empire, as do copies of Plato's *Phaedo* the Academy, and octavo editions of Marx the Communist movement (only by this process can the writings be gathered together, the opus canonized, the words put back into circulation). Because we fetishize memory in its material forms, its facticity causes us to overlook the very materializing organization it was called on to extend in the first place. The doctrine's influence and success wipe clean the memory of indoctrination's painful gestation; opus eclipses operation. *Optimal transmission is transmission forgotten.* Hence the imperative of reminders that go against what is natural in these matters. The fact that the fruit melts so spontaneously into palate's pleasure calls for a more rigorous understanding of the grower's art.

NETWORKS AND TERRITORIES

Transmitting means organizing; it thus stakes out territory. It consolidates a whole, draws borderlines, defends itself, and exiles others ("Unity's nature is exclusion," Bossuet cautioned). The problem with territory is that it is always already there. From its preexistence arises the political effort necessary to dissolve the territorial ties of subjects who have come from elsewhere or from yesterday, before being reterritorialized differently, that is, given a new supraterritorial allegiance. The kind of organization stipulated by Christianity calls for a personalization of belief unprecedented in the antique world (for a Greek or Roman an individual credo has neither meaning nor place). Its effect was to separate the converted from their sociopolitical membership within the *civitas*'s topography of traditions only to enroll them in those created by a new, ecclesiastical territory. There, the less firmly established the church's ties to traditional localities, the tighter and more total its administrative net. For the new laypeople, parishes and dioceses simply took the place of the ancient Attican and Athenian demes and Roman centuries or tribes. Organizing cannot proceed without dividing tasks and demarcating spaces.

A holder of title or office in whom authority has been vested sees to the regulation and administration of the transmitted inheritance, to its proper circulation among the believers (or knowers), and ultimately to the adaptation of both these services to the external milieu. To do this, the useful redundancy of a hierarchized institution is highly recommended. Emile Poulat has insisted on the obscure *commutative* relation between a body of knowledge and a power, between a science and a potential, between a know-what and a know-*how*. Can we not shed light on this relation by seeing it as the effect of the principiative (originative, initiative) relation that joins a memory to a territory; or more broadly, the symbolic to the political?

No territory, ideal or physical, exists without a capital (from *caput*, head). Every school has its headmaster or principal, every doctrine its founder, every county its administrative center, and even Fourier's phalansteries were set up with father-directors. Fortifying a territory also means deposition of doctrine (or with Islam and Judaism, investiture of a sacred language). An orthodoxy is authorized to escort and drive home a founding and appropriately political partition of territory between inside and outside. "To make stable," "to enclose," and "to make faithful" all imply one another. Does not the praise we lavish on the asystematic modern nomad (so frequent among contemporaries) forget that historically the nomad was a conqueror and thus a potential sedentary? All territoriality is organized according to a center that directs and peripheries that undergo. This is the difference in nature between a network (which is technological) and a territory (which remains political).

The capillaceous model of cyberspace communities sometimes relegates the pyramidal or linear model of organizations once wielding authority to the Stone Age. I have my doubts about the results of blindly extrapolating any order of reality into another (however denigrated the more traditional one as "neolithic"). The Internet is a headless network, a decentralized rhizome stretching limitlessly and horizontally. This is why the giddily anarchical World Wide Web, despite the metaphoric momentary highs to which it currently takes us, seems incapable of transmuting the virtual neurons of a planetary brain into the members of a real community of feeling and action. A collective intelligence does not ipso facto produce an elective or electoral solidarity. As data is not knowledge, so a PC is not a polity. Cyberdemocracy is the dream of technocrats who have forgotten their partially animal existence. Only by remaining preoccupied with this latter have those definitive religious or political prophets who are invested with official duties of demarcation ensured their success over time.

The fate of the commons, or *socius*, is territorial, our genealogy as zoological beings contributing to it innately.[5] Large groups' organizational fabric depends on their means of locomotion and mobilization. In my book *L'état séducteur: Les révolutions médiologiques du pouvoir* I sought to delineate those relations that join together technologies for transmitting and institutional forms for governing. It is not hard to appreciate furthermore that cyberspatial information highways do not make for the same kind of empire, give rise to the same kind of metropolitan hegemony, as the metaled or cobblestoned roadbed constructed by human labor. The Roman Empire's static constructedness—pyramidal and radiating outward from the central *Urbs*—and its mania for accumulating and storing are markedly different from the dynamic, mobile, network architecture of the U.S. Empire, in which flows (of capital, goods and services, information, and people) have displaced stockpiles. A network is not a nonterritory but an organized connectedness (a basic definition of the French *réseau*, which was coined at the beginning of the nineteenth century to describe the linked systems of urban waterworks for carrying water and draining sewage). Networks cannot meet the same criteria of practical effectiveness that apply to a simple relation ordered in a single direction.

It would be worth examining, on this score, the discontinuous shift in evolutionary rhythms one observes when moving from the institution responsible for conveyance (organized matter) to its material infrastructure (materialized organization). There is, on the one side, the dynamics of the *quomodo*, the how, of initiation that belongs to technological progress proper and unfolds as a product of numerous human agencies interacting with the materiel. On the other, there is the relative inertia of the *quid*—the agency of the initiating (toward whatever end)—that properly belongs to every group formation. Jewish ritual today observes the same rites, celebrates the same religious holidays, chants the same psalms and to the same swaying of the body that it did three thousand years ago. The *talit*, or prayer shawl, is held in one hand, the *Torah* scroll in the other, as shown on the Wall of Jerusalem. The Roman Catholic Church conserves mindsets and administrative structures inherited from the technological era of Constantine. Believers in information, contemporaries of the atomic age, follow the same liturgical calendar and move among the same mental and physical topography of holy places (Rome, Jerusalem, Santiago de Compostela) as people in the time of windmills and Philip II. They are oriented toward the same space-time coordinates because of a sui generis organization, an *Ekklesia*, that is itself not easily disoriented. This *Ekklesia* has crossed memory's successive technological periods intact, through the letter, the analogue, and the binary code. It is itself a self-reproducing memory, with a supra- or interethnical ethnicity endowed with a vital independence and animate with internal programming like a living being. Even when televangelism made its appearance on the scene of Protestant cultural settings (an example of how new material devices mediate religion's propagation), it did not modify the evangelical canon (the initiating *quid* of collective formations). The mobile array of organized matter innovates while the stationary motor of material organization conserves. But the innovative effort of the evolving technology has a need for organizational stability. To find fault with the pedagogical or religious agents of memory—whether school or denomination, time's gifts for the forgetful—for turning their backs on the present and on modern life is to fail to understand their very reason for being. The school couldn't possibly be ashamed of an attachment to the past so much a part of its very function (and so disruptive of the amnesia induced by commercialism and consumerism). Transmission withers on the vine when the present is taken as the only model. And innovation itself withers with it, scorn for the past being the greatest enemy of progress.

CHRISTIANITY'S MEDIOLOGY

The formation of revealed religions offers an exemplary field of experimentation. It is more rewarding to study than the propagation of secular ideologies spawned during the last century, developments whose timescale is more condensed but whose effects are more superficial (despite all the sound and fury). Did not the organizing of belief in a single God, particularly the evangelical message's multisecular diffusion through Rome's Western world, take to its maximum performance a culture's symbolic efficacy, that is, the production of real, material effects (political, territorial, and administrative) from immaterial givens (words, signs, and images)? Just as the genius of the Incarnation provides a code of intelligibility for studying mediations in history—a kind of mystic calculus—so too the genesis of faith in Christ furnishes my approach with its *via crucis*. This historical genesis attests, better than any other historical experience, to the general truth that *the object transmitted does not preexist the process of its transmission*, if it indeed appears that Christianity invented Christ instead of the other way round.

Is there a more telling sign of the dual nature of the mediating organizational body, of its inherent ambivalence, than the meaning of the Greek word *ekklesia*? In liturgical Greek it designates first the main body of an architectural structure, the physical site as meeting place; then, in the aftermath of this meaning, the institution of grace, the *corpus mysticum* of the Christ. (A similar usage is not immaterial in this respect: do not the terms *cinema* and *theater* suffer, or benefit, from the same equivocation?) Its first version uncapitalized, its second capitalized, *ekklesia* carries the double signification of a single crucial operator—a linking mechanism, like the kingbolt connecting the front and rear axle and wheels of an automobile chassis or the trucks of a railroad car—that proved decisive in the transmission of the message-Messiah (and whose double nature in Jesus as fully man, fully God, founded Christology). "The reason for the Christian faith is that Christ died and regained life" runs the causal argument. The objective validity of this reason counts less to our way of thinking than the fact that its initial, historical stimulus was objectified, formulated, and reformulated by a church that learned to assure its perpetuation across the centuries, down to our own. It is irrelevant to mediology whether Jesus of Nazareth was raised from the dead on the third day; the central question is to know how the tradition that established him was elaborated and carried on. Why is it that Adonis, Attis, and Osiris, eastern mystery cults all, have not come to be worshiped among modern-day celebrants, while the Christian mystery was carried across the centuries? Dwindled and weatherbeaten it may be, yet it is still proclaimed and confessed by communities of the faithful gathering together and setting up churches distributed over five continents two thousand years after the "facts." Unable ever to know if Jesus was brought back to life, we are positive however that people believed it happened. The psychological mechanisms of such a belief are not hard to imagine. Jesus' disciples could not endure the grief of losing him; hope against hope got the better of them, and they saw him alive again in imagination and posited his continued life in heaven. Here is the real miracle of the faith. And here are the grounds to say that the idea of Jesus' heavenly life explains his apparitions on earth and not vice versa. The idea outlived the visions, and faith in the living Christ outlived the particular sightings following his death. How the miracle has been renewed and renewed, making its way to us (witnesses to nothing)—is the central question.

So, yes, the generation of Jesus' apostles has long vanished, in subjection to biological law, but not their belief. It was transmitted to Paul of Tarsus, for instance, someone who did not meet the living Jesus during his ministry yet saw him with his own eyes risen from the dead on the road to Damascus. The converted Paul found ways to convert others, who in their turn forged the chain from age to age, city to city. The articulation of Christian faith turns on solid pivots: on relics, sacred images, and holy scriptures that are directed less toward propagating the *memory* of past words and deeds than the impersonal *interpretation* that the distant alleged witnesses, Matthew, Mark, Luke, and John, are supposed to have given them in their lifetime. Doctrine refers to an admirable propagation of Christianity, adding further cause for believing in it. The mediologist, whether or not a believer, has the task of supplementing admiration with an explanation.

Wherefrom we can deduce that, strictly speaking, there are no "founding key words" or "founding principles" (ill-chosen expressions at best) from which traditions and institutions of transmission originate. A mediological approach would do well to renounce the idealist's illusion that our culture is founded on a few simple formulations or messages that brought about its present state. The institutional body supposed to relay these disembodied word-principles has gradually invented its own origin. The words it is held to have transcribed it was indeed the first to compose. The holy speech of Jesus did not come first, only to be gathered and set down by apostle-mediators subsequently and then finally broadcast on all fronts (*omnes gentes*) by members of the priestly body serving as mere relays. Instituted Christianity uttered the Christian proclamation. "A word become world" has it backward; a world was only uttered through and in the priesthood's speech. Holy writ is produced by particular communities making use of it as needed in order to communify. Hence, in the case of both Christianity and Islam, the belated character of their sacred scripture: following their faith, interpreters still found license, for several centuries, to reinvent after their own fashion the revealed religious texts they claimed only to be quoting verbatim. (Six centuries were needed for the Christian church to adopt and establish the twenty-seven books of the New Testament.)

Likewise is it fitting to take *cum grano salis* the hackneyed expression of historians of philosophy "Plato's 'founding idea' that. . . ." What indeed would Plato have amounted to had he not had the brainstorm of purchasing a plot of land near the Athenian suburb of Colonus where he established a sanctuary of the Muses? This proving ground for the mind, dubbed the Academy, became the collective property—of a school. Plato launched this religious association, and in turn it instituted the thinking of its founder as foundational. What would we have known about Plato's ideas without his nephew and successor, Speusippus?[6] Without Xenocrates and, after him, Polemon?[7] All of them became links in a chain across time and helped build the coherence of a doctrine (and thereby its capacity to *become* doctrine) in rivalry with the organized schools of the Lyceum, the Porticum, and the Garden (each one a territory generating its own war machine).

The disciplines invent the teachers. And, as it turned out, the Neoplatonists —more orthodox even than the direct successors installed in the Academy— invented Platonism. If you wish to understand a theology, examine its corresponding ecclesiology: you will pass from the form to the formative matrix. From the consequence to the cause. The critical agencies of acculturation (into Platonism, religion, Marxism, psychoanalysis, what have you) are bodies rather than spirits. Only bodies can deliver the message. To think is to organize. If you begin by incorporating, the incorporeal will be given to you in the bargain, the line of succession opened unto you. An inheritance is recorded only once you have made the record to which it is owed.

2

Crossroads or Double Helix?

THE TWO LINES

This, then, is the nodal point of my proposed diagram of transmission's criss-crossing lines, the point where organized matter and materialized organization interact, where material base and social relations are in their most dialectical relationship to one another. It is impossible to treat the communitarian level of authority separately from its means for communicating or to treat sociability separately from technicity. If such a vantage point can stake a single claim of originality, it is its refusal to sacrifice either the technical equipment or the institutional group when analyzing the trails left by symbols. What matters most is to travel along the ridge from which both these historical slopes can be scoured. One must take in both the mundane matters of the highway department and the sublimities of the lyre, both civic and literary genius, the laying down of both pipes and party platforms.[1] Transmission's genius is a long ambivalence.

For those with a lingering preference for the genius of Christianity over that of the engineers, it is essential to bring together two etymological ancestries of the word *religion* about which philologists have quarreled since the days of classical antiquity. Authors such as Cicero relate the word to the verb *legere*, "to gather or bring together." Others such as Lactantius and Tertullian argue for *ligare*, "to link together."[2] Does not the one naturally imply the other? Without indeed gathering up saints' relics, without collecting here and there from far away bits and pieces threatened with extinction (the *relegere* part), how is a durable link ever to be forged between contemporaries (the *religare* part)? A scrupulous conservation of traces and a capacity for rallying together, each activity in solidarity with the other, constitute one and the same operative function practicable two ways. Whether or not they derive from individuals' particular confessions of faith, the ties that bind those individuals in depth depend on their confidence in some external symbol, a jointly held factor x. A formal axiom holds that community lies only at the foot of the edifice of symbolism overseeing it.

As things now stand, we are struggling to overcome the separateness of the two cultures that, comfortably set in their ways, preside over the jurisdictions of knowledge. Within the human sciences, each specialization partakes of the conveniences and indolence of insularity. Barring a miraculous departure from custom, historians and sociologists (who specialize in the study of materialized organization) turn their backs on technological circles of activity and the devices used in different periods for recording and organizing human memory, from systems of writing to the national highway system, from our tools of inscription to our habits of touring and circuits of travel. They study institutions, collapse the history of ideas into that of so-called great works and doctrines, and remain exegetes. Specialists in organized materialities—scholars of the history of technology and of memory machines and observers of material culture—do the opposite. Often they bracket institutional questions and the parameters of social or political history. Under the rubric of technological history, the invention of pendulums and escapements for mechanical clocks, say, will be anatomized (as in the work of David Landes). The philosophy rubric generates treatises on being and time and Heideggerian phenomenologies of lived temporality. The paths taken by these two kinds of researchers are averse to intersecting.

The one camp will follow the trajectory of processes of mechanical reproduction and printing while the other traces that of religiosity in the West. One side details the nineteenth century's epic of road and rail construction; the other, the republicans' inroads in the French provinces. For the political historians, it is as though the modes of political domination were somehow independent of the ways of handling geographic distances and time delays. As if a given political culture were not first of all a distinct technological culture, or as if the civic sensibilities of a contemporary were unrelated to his preferred toolkit of accoutrements for influencing people and decisions. (Is not the republican politician, more adept at the unspontaneous delayed broadcast, also a bibliomaniacal mincer of words on paper? And is not today's democrat a swimmer in the audiovisual flow of sound and images? The first one will send you a letter, while the second will call you on the phone.) Political history continues to isolate politics from technics as if the size of sovereign spaces were not a function of communications and the networks of rail-, road-, and waterways available to transport. (Did not the transnational highway system contribute as much to "building one Europe" as the Brussels Commission? Will not the interuniversity *Numeris* network add more to the consciousness of European unity than the intergovernmental agreements concluded in high quarters?) As if our present policies of humanitarian diplomacy and our legislation that has written intervention into law were not the implacable result of live satellite and radio coverage abroad, as oblivious to borders as it is to international law. As if the nature of the social bond, anywhere, could have nothing to do with the instrumental braiding together of human aggregates. And as if there were no coinciding at all between mediological revolutions and political turning points, between the Phoenician invention of the vocalic alphabet and the emergence of the Greek city, between Gutenberg's printing press and Luther's Reformation, the industrialization of the book and the formation of national consciousness, political journalism and the parties of notables, Marinoni's rotary press and the expansion of mass party politics.

We expect the citizen to be well instructed in the laws that she or he arranges to have taught. Thus every major reshuffling of technologies of the letter—in rough chronological order, artisanal, industrial, and (intangibly) electronic—means a corresponding change of saddle for the citizenry. This pervasive material conditioning may seem to take place at the lowly level of the roadbed or even underground, but this does not rule out the new technological protocols' sublimation into a regulating ideal by the metamorphosis of procedural necessity into obligatory forms of social interaction. For the Athenian city-state, the idea model was *orthographical*: the letter of the law, etched onto a stele that all could read, made possible reciprocal supervision between citizens and representatives, contrary to the aristocratic orality of Sparta. For the Enlightenment, the model was *typographical*, following Kant's definition of the public use of Reason as the person whom one styles as knowledgeable before the totality of the reading public. For the Second and Third French Republics, it was *bookish and schoolish*, with that period's extended projects of permanent civic education (from primary school to popular adult education, taken up under the Fourth and Fifth Republics as *l'action culturelle*) and its goal of democratizing knowledge so as to split up power. Public space can be conceived as that space where written utterances circulate under certain concrete conditions that are rarely, if ever, thematized (stationers, delivery of mail, roadways, railways, customs seals, typesetting, etc.). A modification of the networks of communication has the effect of altering ideas. The electromagnetic telegraph, for instance, dynamized the republican structuring of the state; television tends to shatter it. To cite another example, de Gaulle might well have been vanquished by the redoubtable forces evoked in Napoleon's remark, "There is more reason to dread the hostility of three newspapers than a thousand bayonets," if his solemn and authoritative "voice of France" had not managed to drown out the grumblings of critics who depended exclusively on the written word. Could not a political history of France or the United States be written by evoking in historical succession, to borrow from Woody Allen's terms, their newspaper days, radio days, and TV days?

Opinions about the means and pervasive emissions of mass communication today are distributed between two continents. Optimism prevails to the west of the Atlantic, a certain pessimism to the east. There would seem to be a face-off between a European line and an American line (however many complicated provenances, exiles, and mixed breeds one might also identify). Is not the first line philosophical, critical, and generalizing; the second, empirical, quantitative, and microtargeted? Doubtlessly so, yet the cultivation of aprioristic explanations and each line's territorialism are antagonistic only superficially. The American approach bubbles with energy and sings of cybertech liberation, while the more nostalgic European one mourns a loss. Might we call this match the Manic meets the Melancholic?

Indeed, Europe favors the more *political* moment of cultural transmission (the Frankfurt school's critical theory is emblematic here). A mistrustful deconstruction uncovers the ideological manipulation and social control behind the equipment of cultural production, so many instruments of enframing and subjugation. Communication is instrumentalized by domination. In this political totalism, the strategic intent of the engineers and mechanics dissolves or neutralizes all constraints that otherwise might belong to the machinery itself (networks, material base of inscription, devices). The culture industries' internal logic, as Edgar Morin showed a while back, implies, however, a promotion of what is singular, shocking, indeed abnormal, so that the stereotypical consumer takes in a steady and random diet of manufactured prototypes of novel experience (films, music, dress, etc.). The conformity machine thrives on uniform anticonformity; only by keeping outside the paradox of serialized originals can one reduce the forms of mass media to their single leveling function. The European Grand Intellectual denounces the culture industry as a factor in mindless conformity, cultural decline, and one-dimensional mass inhumanity. Guardians of the highest literary and philosophical culture, Adorno and Horkheimer (the notion's inventor), are scornful of film, jazz, and radio.

Pierre Bourdieu tries the case of television. These pessimistic inheritors of the Enlightenment mean to demystify the anti-Aufklärung applications of an instrument that by their lights could be put to better uses in more capable hands. Their humanist diatribes against industrial alienation are animated by a classically instrumental view of technology conceived as the sum of mere props and nonessential tools at the disposal of a cause that far surpasses them. With his concept of mechanical reproduction as degradation of the original's aura, Walter Benjamin belongs fully to this grand lineage, although he is both more artistic and more genuinely inquisitive vis-à-vis the innovations of his time.

As befits a nation of engineers and pioneers of industry, the American line favors instead transmission's *technologic* moment. Its media are the message. From Edison to Bill Gates and Bell to Nicholas Negroponte, there has been an implacable drive to pare down communicative devices and systems to their intrinsic properties. This postulates the political neutrality of the media of emission, just as the European line postulated the neutrality of technologic media. It overlooks ideological tendentiousness in order to talk performance. The effective functions of the tool, as well as the ulterior imperial motives of the operators, are all absorbed and concealed by the tool's potential, abstract deployments. Good news about the newest conduit, channel, or network of civilization-as-content-provider, occludes the nature of information spew itself and how it might enslave its human receivers. Transmission via satellite, we are told, obsolesces the nation-state and political rivalries of yore. Yet territorial disputes are replaced by wars between competitors about norms, the euphemistic technological equivalent of nationalist expansionism. This heralded rejection of ideology turns exorbitantly ideological in reality. We see it break out in today's euphoria of exaltations over the Web and information superhighway as paths to salvation. Digital interconnectedness for everyone is offered up as the newest panacea, leading to no less than a planetary blossoming of democratic individualism. Being counted part of the network as an imaginary cure for the ills of exclusion casts the chill of a technologic asepsis onto what is hotter matter: the *political* question, proper and improper. The American line of approach to transmission does tend to dominate more fully when it dissociates communication from domination by secluding normalization behind machines and equipment, in all their deceptive fascination.

On the European side, political realism is allied with technological angelism; on the American, political angelism with technological realism.[3] Such symmetry, which holds at the thematic level, fails however at the level of surface coverage. (Nor of course does it apply to the matter of intellectual coherence: pitting Adorno against Bill Gates mixes apples and oranges.) Given the eviction of politics by the business and government administrator, the fecundity of research labs, and the huge shift of the United States' winds of change from a westerly to an easterly direction, the last two decades have put the European line in the minority even in Europe. It would be a shame to react by buttressing oneself on traditional European-line arguments prioritizing domination in order to thwart the American-line hegemony prioritizing communication. It is better to refuse such an alternative by both technicizing the political factor and politicizing the technical factor at the outset. By way of further illustration: "America" reflects primarily on the roadway and the cable while "Europe" gives thought to the missionary or the message. Our rule of thumb will be Euro-American: we must put the pilgrim back on the pavement.[4]

THE TRAGEDY OF TRANSMISSION

Toward the last century's close a certain romanticism rethought more deeply the bittersweet material constraints of perpetuation. Maurice Maeterlinck lamented that Nature dictates we die at the moment we transmit life. Edward von Keyserling observed that the flame only brightens and gives off heat by consuming its own substance. The philosopher and sociologist Georg Simmel (1858–1918) coined the phrase "tragedy of culture" to express how vital force, to realize itself in the world, has need of its own antithesis, which makes it die. The rigidity of concepts and norms blocks and enfeebles a surge of spirit that, did it not infix and entrench itself within the objective limits of a given form, would never be prolonged. So it goes with every cultural emission's prolongation: things and people to relay its work must be carried on by institutions that soon become fixed into exclusive, normative, dogmatic, ritualistic, corporate societies. Immanent to the affirmation of a cultural value is its negation.

Did not this immanence of death to life find its canonical representation in the Christian myth of the Incarnation, also a superlative emblem of profane mediations? Manifesting itself in the flesh, in order for it to happen as a presence amid humankind, the Word was held to make itself vulnerable to shedding tears of blood and to giving up the ghost that it might one day come back transfigured among men and women, according to the plan of providential salvation. If, fallen on the ground, the grain did not die, it would bear no fruit.[5] The evangelical parable of dying to live not only summons the faithful toward a germinative patience and humility but reminds them as well that the tree shall appear fully otherwise from the sown seed or, in different terms, that the outcome of a process of transmission does not bear the characters of the initial message. Tending to the growth of an idea, of whatever kind, *begins by altering it* or deforming it in order to reform it in some fashion. As the Nativity, the Passion, and the Resurrection are rolled out into a concrete chain of transmission, a modicum of order is salvaged from a cruel succession of disorders. Along with or in spite of its heavy burden of suffering, the Christian Resurrection carries across with optimal efficacy its transmission of victory over death. It is an ideal allegory of a very real historical mutation, one that is sometimes additive, sometimes disfiguring, but never passive or repetitive.

Transport *by* is transformation *of*. That which is transported is remodeled, refigured, and metabolized by its transit. The receiver finds a different letter from the one its sender placed in the mailbox. *Traddutore, traditore.* To trans*mit* should not be considered merely to trans*fer* (a thing from one point to another), any more than cultural inheriting should be deemed a mere instance of receiving (it is rather a process of selecting, reactivating, and recasting). To reinvent and thus modify: why?

The answer is: because the transmitted information is not independent of its double medium, technological and organic, especially the latter. In a sense, the term in French for the material base of a message, that which receives its trace, preserves it, and conveys it—*le support*—proves signally inapt. It postulates too restrictively a relation of exteriority between the thing carried and that on which it rests, as the table supports the tureen of soup on its surface. Transmission of a meaning-content in fact incorporates the meaning into its vehicle, submits it to the vehicle's own law of behavior. It is, after all, mediation's *substantial* character that sets transmission going as a transubstantiation, a dynamical transmutation not a mechanical reproduction, that truly adds on as much as it takes away. That is to say, there is not, on one side, memory and, on the other, forgetting. Loss binds with the very act of recalling and recollecting; alteration is conservation's other face. Everything gets conserved, as it were, and nothing does, as well; these two activities are moreover identical. Antoine Berman writes of seeing the rule of an "innovative entropy or entropic innovation" at work when one language is translated into another. Can such a rule not be applied to every production of meaning sent hurtling into time "like the seed at the blowing wind's whim."[6] Often this entropy is the flip side of an antientropic force, for the organization that ceaselessly reorganizes its patrimony does generate order, but its *own* order, the order imposed by its own perpetuation, which reconfigures the legacy it preserves to the specifications of its peculiar circumstances. This entropy too can be the outcome of a saturation and not also of an amputation. Sometimes overwatering the soil dries it out. Witness how disintegrated memories can become as a result of traces piling up, how knowledge can give out under an information deluge, in today's hypermediated societies where too many messages discourage all retention.

Incarnation never promised happiness. It is diametrically opposite the idea of kitsch, in which the positive wins without any negative. To the smiley schmaltz of stardom it prefers the sadness and humility of the Madonna's smile through tears, radiant in grief. There can be no salvation without embodiment, none either without sin. True, pace good Pauline theology (and Saint Paul was the quintessential incarnator of the Christian idea), the flesh is the *seat* and not *cause* of sin, prelapsarian Adam not having been pure spirit, as neither was the young Jesus. Still, at the same time that the Christian body can bring salvation and liberation, it cannot fully extricate itself from its Greek fate as *sôma sèma*: the body as tomb and prison. That great early mediologist standing before the eternal and rhymer of *incarnation* with *incarceration*, Charles Péguy, never stopped meditating on this terrible mystery. The author of *Notre jeunesse* lived out and described "the republican mystique's degradation into republican politics," not in the terms of a scandalous experience but as the expression among others of a natural law he formulated as, "*Everything* begins in mysticism and ends up as politics." The decline and weakening inherent in materially transferring traditions inscribe, as part of the agenda, a refill, a recharging, every day that God makes. This latter countertransference is necessary so that "the mystical not be devoured by the very politics it brought into the world," a Sisyphean task that already makes up by itself an entire politics, the crux of political work.

This Christian poet identified perfectly what constitutes a "revolution in thought." It is hardly a thing of astounding cleverness:

> In this order of reality, the question is not one of cleverness. It is simply one of an idea, at a certain moment of the world's history, making its entrance "into." The greatest revolutions, in all kinds of orders of

existence, were not made with and by extraordinary ideas, and it even belongs to genius to proceed by means of the simplest ideas. Only in very ordinary times do simple ideas wander around like dreamy phantoms. When a simple idea takes bodily form, there is a revolution. . . . Everything is in the incorporation, in the incarceration, in the incarnation. . . . Everything is in the integration, and it is extremely rare. Of God there was but a single incarnation, and even of ideas there are well nigh very few incorporations. . . . And History can count only three or four of these great, earthshaking transformations.[7]

The Christian religion was one such great seismic rattling, of course. So too was communism, on a smaller and more precarious scale, in this century. Hence the mediologist's interest in these long cultural shakeups that conducted their experiments with incarnation-incarceration outside the test tube and the laboratory.

What diligent laborer, speeding his plow in his own field of competency and reflecting on the times and his parish, has not, at some moment, repeated inwardly the wisdom behind Alfred Loisy's observation about the development of early Christianity, "It was the Christ whose return they were awaiting: the Church showed up instead"? For those who remain on the doorstep, unwilling to come inside as members and take to heart the formalized manner in which an idea has been suddenly taken seriously only to truly shake the world with its ramifications, there is no more absorbing, chronic, or deplorable state of mind than when one is forced to compare the goodness of the original pronouncements with the utter noxiousness of the institutions derived from them. The theological children of Abraham—whom the hermeneutics of sacred texts would distract from observing profane processes (processes of which the Scriptures are a result and not the source, being produced by a retroactive refashioning)—are not the least disheartened and sincere. They speak of the Bible, the Gospels, or the Koran as eloquent pleas for life, for love, for fraternity. And the established religions professing them commit acts of extermination and fratricidal murder. These religions have brought in their train exclusion, hierarchy, and simplistic arguments based on authority: "This is scandalous. People will not desist from betraying the word of God (or the Prophet, or the Messiah)." Whence comes this feeling of being scandalized? In large part from juxtaposing the *initial* (or what one presumes to be) state of the line of transmission with its *terminal* state, while omitting both the middle-ground transformations and the process understood as a whole. The very thing that morally appalls the orphan of historic origins might also intellectually summon the mediologist. In his view of things, it is the undue neglect of mediations and of the constraints attending collective formation that transforms a poorly understood metamorphosis into a much-reviled contradiction between ideal and real. For lack of wanting to investigate the logic of logistics, the believer offers outcries of indignation, which can be the first step toward denouncing scapegoats. The mediologist is content with plausible, if painstaking, reconstruction. And with even-handed understanding.

3

The Exact Science of Angels

A VENERABLE PROTOMEDIOLOGY

The type of inquiry put forward in this book actually has nothing novel about it. Nothing, that is, that has not been better expressed in various idioms and systems from earliest time.

The act of carrying a message or announcing important news was signified in Greek by the verb *angelein*. The messenger or delegate was called *angelos*. Though it falls to the angels to be the bearers of good news, one should avoid forgetting Rilke's warning, in the opening lines of the second Duino elegy, about that strange bird of disaster:

Every angel is terrifying. And yet the woe is mine;
I sing to you, almost deadly birds of my soul,
Knowing what you are.[1]

[Jeder Engel ist schrecklich. Und dennoch, weh mir,
ansing ich euch, fast tödliche Vögel der Seele,
wissend um euch.]

Angels do not exist, it would seem. No more in heaven than on earth. A statement indeed likely to be true. And yet it has already been demonstrated (by Lévi-Strauss) that man objectifies his thought in his myths, and the first religious mythologies suggest a pre-science of man in his infancy, babbling in figures and metaphors. Early Christian theology can and should be read, at least by nonbelievers, as anthropology untamed. And angelology in particular should be read as mediology in a mystic or nebulous state. It will be my concern, under the neologism of mediology, to take up and clarify, in the terms of the here-below, the details of a task learnedly undertaken long ago, so to speak, in the clouds: the anatomy and taxonomy of angels.

Doubtless the angel beings of Europe's childhood lack the structuralist prestige of New Guinea's totems, and church history does not have the exotic charms of the myths of the Dakota analyzed by Malinowski or Lévi-Strauss. Anthropologists have been granted license to elaborately scrutinize bear and sturgeon legends among the Manamini Indians or other reincarnation myths of eagles transformed into men prevalent among Hopi clans using wild mustard. Why not extend the same documentary value, when it comes to the human mind, to old tales of dragons and bird-men in medieval Europe? It is more difficult to become an ethnologist of the domestic beliefs of Europe's past. But let us suppose the history of religions that have structured great civilizations and been tested by time to contain as much information about the laws of nature and society as one can find in Eskimo or Polynesian myths. There is nothing innately absurd in proceeding from such an assumption.

In every written record that we can consult within the branch of Roman Catholic theology called angelology can be found the three properties of transmission as a historical process: first, a triadic structure that brings in a third mediating term, between a message's emission and its reception; second, a structured order that makes *organization* synonymous with *hierarchy*; and third, a reversal scheme that switches passage into obstacle. The intransitive character of the mechanics of messaging and the inexorable nature of the interface can be identified with the impossibility of a direct face-to-face meeting between God and sinners. The hierarchical ordering of a corps of mediators can be found in the properly military chain of command of the celestial militia. And a tragic reversal scheme lies behind the angel's transposition into demon.

Before taking up these structures at greater length, it is worth recalling that the science of angels served an eminently pragmatic concern (much more typically Roman than Byzantine): managing the conjunctive function. Those who showed the most interest in the sexual gender of angels, for example, were not the dreamers and quibblers of Christian doctrine (the Almighty's petty telegraphers) but rather the decision makers, the grand planners, the virtuosi of the art of giving orders. Classifying the exact status of beings neither fish nor fowl is among the most pedestrian of practical concerns. And time after time, in every school of thought—atheistical or faithful, socialist or liberal-bourgeois—angel*ism* ironically cares little about actual angels. So as realists on the lookout for disguised materialism, let us observe their behavior absolved of the need to draw the veil over our eyes.

GO-BETWEENS

The more speculative a doctrine, the less preoccupied it will be with its administrators and intermediaries. It is the business of government people to fulfill those roles. And thinkers of the first rank (or of the first generation) are of the same mind about disdaining the question of such functions as second order. To give serious thought to the enactor of a message means attending to the *party* or communicative apparatus when one is trying to put across a social project; it means attending to the *church* when the message concerns salvation; and it means attending to *images* when one is primarily an idea or concept person. All these have to do with the means of implementation and with getting messages across: clearing a path or road means giving thought to the bridge. Conscious reflection about these matters is something none of the standard socioprofessional categories (including inventors of doctrine, prophets, philosophers, and engineers of the so-called *service vicinal*, the administration of secondary roads) do spontaneously.

Given that the invention of angels answered a preoccupation with defining and exerting hegemony, it comes as no surprise that Christian angelology was shaped at a moment of ecclesiastical rigidification, in the midst of an institutional normalization of the state religion in 391 A.D. It coincided with the appearance of the first monastic barracks in Egypt and Gaul, Tabennesi and Lerins (fourth and fifth centuries), the promulgation of rules of faith, the laying down by official council of sacerdotal lines of command. It is no surprise, either, that the most renowned of the angelologists, Dionysius the Areopagite, passed or was able to pass for such a long time as the disciple and heir of Saint Paul (an institutional creature if ever there was one). It is to Paul that we owe the first hierarchy of the ministries (apostles, prophets, and doctors of the church) as well as a justification of the remove between apostles and peoples using as model the subordination of members of the human body to one another. Those men of the church who made the most of their veneration of angels were all founders of an order or "generals," from Gregory the Great to Loyola, and including the saints Bernard and Benignus. They were all heroes of pastoral service just as (if one adjusts for context a little) in the case of the worker's movement, where the socialist Jules Guesde (1845–1922) and Lenin served as de facto "angelologists" for the deceased Karl Marx. Whatever they might transmit, it was not the doves but the hawks who wondered systematically about the angels or about their secular substitutes, our numerous channels of communication.

Lesson 1: A crowd throngs the monotheistic heaven one might otherwise suppose vacant. In the sixth chapter of Genesis we first learn of "the sons of God" who "saw that the daughters of men were fair; and they took to wife such of them as they chose" (6:2). Commentators have identified these mysterious beings with angels of the heavenly court. The text surprises twice: there is both flesh in the Kingdom of Spirit and multiplicity surrounding the holy One. It is as though God's power were not sufficient unto itself. He personally is *not* the one who alerts the Egyptian servant Agar that she will give birth to Ishmael, who informs Abraham he will father a son with Sarah, who appears to David, who answers lost Esdras's call in Babylon, or who guides the Hebrews in their wanderings. Nor is Allah the one who dictates verses to Mohammed. Moses himself receives the tablets of the Law by the angels' intermediary agency. It is as if God could or would not intervene directly in our affairs. There comes between Him and his prophets themselves an indispensable interpreter-designate—*malak* in Hebrew, *angellos* in Greek—the bearer of a message, carrier of an authorization: Michael, Gabriel, Uriel, or some other subordinate commander. Agar, Lot, Gideon, and the others have their dealings only with ministers of the divine government, representatives to, ambassadors sent by a president whose presence no foreign national can perceive through the senses. So too, in the New Testament, do vital messengers intercede to tell Joseph he must flee into Egypt, Mary that she will conceive and learn about the Word's conception in her womb, the magi that they will be led to the stable, and the holy women that they will discover Christ's empty sepulcher the day of the Resurrection (one of the official miracles at which there was no witness present). John of Patmos, author of the book of Revelation, or the Apocalypse (unveiling), makes it known that nobody beholds God directly. Sight of him, face to face, is to be the final recompense for souls in Heaven, their beatific vision. Until that time—Kafka's *The Castle* of course comes to mind—the supreme authority, inaccessible and impenetrable, expresses himself by surrogates speaking in his name, enigmatically.

In this way, nothing on high or here below, or (even less so) on the elevator trips between floors, can unfold with transparency and immediacy. This is far indeed from the automatic evidence of a do-it-yourself transaction or a personal management of one's fate. The decrees of the Almighty are not issued in real time and like an open book. They take their course in a temporal progression for which nothing is played out ahead of time. Providence depends on an economy of implementation. The Nativity necessitates an Annunciation; the Ascension, forty days after Easter, has to have its lifts. The Son of God himself, in the Scriptures and representations, cannot reach his father in heaven minus the help of thousands of winged carriers, whom he still needs even when rising gloriously above the heavenly choirs. This is to say nothing of the Virgin Mary's similar Assumption. No biblical personae make their exit on their own. The Eternal One moreover provides for each of us a guardian angel, as well as, for each nation, an *archon* (from Greek "ruler"), who acts as a guide assigned to its every move. Saint Michael, of all archangels the most frequently called on, was Israel's guardian, and he traditionally passes for being that of France.

It was only when the absolute took refuge in the abstract, with monotheism, that the figure of the intercessor became ineluctable. God's absence-presence had to be bridged by an imagistic interface between invisible divinity and our downcast eyes of flesh and blood. In the same way that the imaginative faculty overrides the Kantian separation between the intelligible and the sensible, the angel became a necessary monstrosity, a fantasy rigorously accounted for. Without recourse to it, the primordial creative force, itself uncreated, could quite simply not have made itself understood and recognized by its creatures. A ransom was paid for the creation of God in the form of a bustling ferment of androgynes, hybrids, or, in Platonist lingo, *metaxú* neither fully incarnate nor discarnate. The ambivalence of their interface is hard to conceptualize but easier to depict; it favors more an iconography than an axiomatics, coming nearer to poetics than logic. Angels make possible a quotidian contact between infinite and finite, divine and human, spirit and matter: they are impossible constitutionally yet indispensable politically.

Christian doctrine was not uniform in its sensitivities to the needs angels fulfilled. Gnosticism, which calibrated salvation on the degree of knowledge but confined itself with a too abstract logic to the conceptual divorce between two orders of reality, came close to an intellectualist or purist parti pris. It could barely accommodate the marvelous, music and stained glass windows, the familiar, the impure, and the transitions of affect. By its logic, the Perfect One takes part in divine realities without making use of intermediaries, priests and sacraments, representations and guardian angels. Nor did this heresy have a place for a Long Church beyond the smaller elite of the elect. Lacking *putti*, winged androgynes, and dragons with claws, Gnosticism (as Marx might have said via Lenin and the propaganda experts) failed to take hold of the masses to become a material force.

The philosophers' God also can dispense with angels, images, and even church. Spinoza's God is the absolutely infinite being, his own cause, outside of whom nothing can exist. This idea of an *Ens perfectissimum* is certainly clever, but it has never amounted to a real weltanschauung, never held people under its contagious spell or warmed them at a hearth that could also become the hotbed of a resistance movement. It would seem that the worshipful gesture, the empty (metaphysical) piety, of an omnipotent pantheistic God—a God shorn of prostheses, of the props and crutches needed to approach him—could not be sustained at such distance. Keeping such faith is like hanging a door without hinges or speaking vocabulary without syntax.

It falls to the simpler souls of Christian faith to improve the aim of those learned doctors who have always trained a suspicious eye on the bastard creatures that are the angels, these disruptive annoyances whom the purist has no qualms about denouncing as a backslide toward polytheism, a reversion to Assyrio-Babylonian magic, a regrettable foreign influence. The books of the Old Testament prior to the Babylonian captivity in fact make no mention of the angels by name; similarly, the devil remains anonymous in those pages and without personalized manifestations, aside from rather vague ones as the serpent. Abbadon, Asmodeus, Satan will all arrive late on the scene. The Book of Job attributes directly to God the agency of disease, afflictions, and death, and the devil does not appear under the name *diabolos* until the belated translation of the Bible into the Greek of the Septuagint. Saint Paul too was skeptical about the cult of angel adoration.[2] For whoever heralds Jesus as the sole mediator of salvation—the *kerygma* proper to Christian belief—angels are of course a dangerous topic. Yet the Nativity, which should have done away with the need for angelic missions from heaven within the Christian economy of salvation, failed to sweep them away. The one and only mediator that is the Christ still had need of ministers and messengers, the couriers between high and low. Angels remained associated with all the sacraments of the faithful, with the church itself, and with each individual. The return of the angels is the return of the monotheistic repressed.

These winged minions having sneaked back in through Christianity's back door and in numerous representations, even speculative theology was unable to do without them for very long. Though toleration of images of divinity came belatedly (at the end of the fourth century), the skittishness of the scholars toward it was undone—and with considerable mediological confidence—by widespread practices of representation and worship. The first Christian art propitiated optical libido by drawing on the decorative pagan repertory. It borrowed from classical *Victories* and *Nikes* (those winged women crowning the victorious), from *amors*, from Roman *genii* (attendant spirits or tutelary deities) bearing the palm leaf and crown on sarcophagi and pegs. It was by these routes that an antique visual model, from the fifth century on, was joined to a textual ready-made from the Bible to lend heavenly spirits the bodily attributes of bird-men they have kept ever since and that we encounter still, atop monumental columns and on movie screens, in the mythological genie of the place de la Bastille or the winged ephebi of Cocteau, Pasolini, and Wenders. Their frothy, billowy hordes in a thousand hues, blossoming in medieval miniatures and quattrocento frescoes, thus defied our logical categories. Pious figuration had the jump on bookish conceptualization (the image gets to things before the idea can). And it indeed proved necessary for men of dogmas and theses to catch up to those who worked in images. It was a pathway that, in Christianity's aftermath, every profane political theory of an excluded third term was obliged to relearn.

ANGELS, PRESENT!

Lesson 2: Every property of the angelic body corporate was open to doubt by the doctors of the church except one: graduation into successive tiers, gradation as if into military echelons. These fluttering acrobats did not just spiral in the ether. They were "incarnadine." No free electrons here; to each its rank, seat, degree, army style. Angels are famous for their smiles; they have seduced the poets. But "den Engel Ordnungen" (Rilke) concerns men of order. It is understood that demons are ranked in a military organization. More surprising and richer in meaning is the idea of an original militarization of creatures symbolizing fluidity, sweetness, and pacifism. A tragic coincidence is that the operative mechanism carrying out conversion from one level of reality to another—here, from supernatural to natural—brings about *subordination*. The meaning of *order* cuts both ways. From the very start, because of its properties that are intrinsically comparative, that is, relative *to* (beneath God, above men; more material than the former and less than the latter), the angel connoted position and place within a preestablished, immobile order. The stray references to angel hierarchy in the Old Testament and in Saint Paul (Ephesians 1:21; Colossians 1:16) broaden into full flower in the works of an Eastern theologian who wrote in Greek sometime during the later fifth and early sixth centuries: Pseudo-Dionysius, known as the Areopagite.[3]

It is to him in *The Celestial Hierarchy* and *The Divine Names* that we owe a systematization that sets up correspondences between ecclesiastical and angelic hierarchies. Dionysius arranges the Army of Good into battle rankings of choirs in descending order of closeness to God, according to the famous *Taxis*. In direct relation with God are seraphim, cherubim, and thrones. Next come dominions, virtues, and powers, which must pass through the first choir. Last, are the principalities, archangels, and angels (lowly soldiers of the celestial militia, at the very bottom of the dignities). Actually, even the seraphim never reach the intimate secrecy of God, which remains fundamentally incomprehensible.

Let us leave aside the question of whether this subordination scheme creates thoroughgoing differences of nature or simple functional ones between the angels of the three classes, the question of criteria for dividing them up and for eventual promotions. Methodius conceived the angels as assigned for all time to their home rank. Augustine, more cautious, offers no opinion. But all the church fathers recognize an arrangement in descending sequence.

Dionysius likewise distinguishes three rankings for ecclesiastical instructors: bishops, priests, and deacons. The people of the initiate are divided into catechumens at the very bottom; energumens, baptized but still under the sway of the devil; and penitents, baptized and on the way toward purity. Within this triadic structure, borrowed from Plato and the cosmologists of antiquity, Christ is the first hierarch, the origin point of the two mutually mirroring hierarchies, celestial and terrestrial. The latter hierarchy, the sacerdotal, was in fact much more complex, as the *Apostolic Constitutions* make clear. After deacons came subdeacons, readers, cantors, ascetics, deaconesses, virgins, widows, and—finally—the people. But the trinitarian model, a required paradigm, served as a triptych framing the smaller frames. The nine choirs were the Trinity multiplied by itself, structuring the series fractally. Dionysius perhaps felt it necessary to ward off an insubordination, to control a zone of instability, by emphasizing the values of classification and stability against anarchy and chaos, afoot or aflight at the edges of this unknown quantity. For the angel is also a counterpower. It fluctuates unpredictably, uncontrollably, insolently with respect (and possible disrespect) to the established magistracy. This airborne switching system connecting man with God short-circuits the more roundabout chain of delegation, necessary links of hierarchical communication. Traveling back and forth, every angel is a potential antipope. Into the ear of a simple follower of the faith he can whisper that the pope is an idiot or the bishop a simonist. Fanaticism with wings offers the desperate a recourse of hope, outside the fossilized ecclesiastic enclave. Witness Joan of Arc.

This Neoplatonist's feet, then, were planted firmly on the ground. He made it his concern to know who the president will be, who would preach in the name of all the others, who would be primus inter pares within the Sacred College or elsewhere, and who within the diocese would be able to consecrate whom. Dionysius the visionary was preoccupied with the serious business of intendancy.

The Alexandrian vision of the world had been haunted by solar metaphors. Dionysian taxonomy absorbed them, but by dint of his ordered deleveling of the illuminators, the scheme of transmission sidestepped the conventional figurations of emanation and diffusion off which rationalistic idealism has fed up to our own day.[4] It was a grand discovery: the intransitive organization of transmission's operators. In this, the highly spiritualistic Dionysius far surpassed in realism the *omne bonum est diffusivum sui* of the scholastics as well as the Enlightenment's lightweight optimism (traces of which can still be found in the prose of UNESCO's charter.) Knowledge by illumination from a light supposed immaterial could be expected to spread naturally across space and time, undividedly. It would propagate in a continuous stream. But Dionysian angels were if anything *spectral*, distributed along (or up and down) a kind of Jacob's ladder whose rungs by definition articulate a discontinuity, an ordered succession of intervals. The art of intervals is common to music and politics. In practice it makes for tonal music theory but also etiquette, melodies as well as jealousies. The angel with harp or viola plucks or strums out notes across a span of equidistant strings. Angels playing their instruments, like the seating in public stands and galleries, are distributed in equidistant rows. Need we recall that ceremonial protocols in the political sphere as well come down to us directly from heaven through the cultural intervention of Byzantium?[5]

A dialectical materialist of the old school will not hesitate to detect in angelic hierarchy a fantastic projection of the terrestrial prototype of imperial houses. But quarreling over chicken and egg seems irrelevant here. What matters is knowing not the thing of which each order is the image but the structure of an order repeated indefinitely "on earth as it is in heaven." The Marxist is free to brand Dionysius a prefeudal ideologue of serfdom, drawing his mystifications from decadent Neoplatonism's kit bag of mischief. I prefer to see in him a researcher in political science (before the discipline came into being) who both anticipated and occulted in mystic ciphers the depressing permanence of hierarchy. We are obliged to acknowledge no single organized society, be it Judeo-Christian, democratic, and even officially egalitarian, that does not present a meticulous inequality in its organs of leadership and executive power, as well as a rigorously defined procession from superior to inferior in its ceremonies and rituals. The more a collective order aspires to be organic, the more it will mark distances between its members in its ceremonials and chains of command. The more closely it might want to follow Saint Paul (and his idea that though being several we are yet one body, members of each other), the more it will be, paradoxically, hierarchized. Hierarchy's undoing of equality is all the more emphatic down below, as the founding transcendence is elevated high above, at the tip of the pyramid of beings. The organization of the Roman Catholic Church—an absolute monarchy of divine right if ever there were one—vividly illustrates this simple-minded if tenacious correlation. It doubtlessly throws light too on the longevity of this institution (and on the incomparable stability of the Vatican state).

A musical overture, an inspired prelude, Dionysian thinking lifted up a corner of the curtained Absolute. Mediation is not horizontal, he glimpsed; every mediation straight away is termed a *procession*—either upward or downward (*anagôgic* or *paradosic*). The introduction of gradients or levels makes every tradition function. Tradition becomes understandable as what is passed on through relay, from master to disciple, student to teacher, son to father, people to apostle. Angels form the chain, yes, but on the condition that its links not all be at the same level. The first, or seraphic, order knows proximity to God; the last, or angelic, verges on the human. God is supported by the top of the ladder, as we the sinners lean on the bottom. Take away the ladder hypothetically, and the terms of the relation disappear with it. The divinization of intelligence or man's union with God—which are the end of every hierarchical activity—cannot come about in a trice, in a single leap out of obscurity into the Light. More than a simple social setting or exoteric framework for an individual illumination, hierarchy inspires, conditions, and acts as impetus for transmitting grace. It is, with Dionysius, the very manifestation of the divine: "deiformity." If there is no hierarchy, God does not exist. But when hierarchy *is* present, God becomes inaccessible. The signal degrades as it passes through the channel. Aptitude for receiving the divine message experiences entropy with the receiver's degree of distance from the sender. "In proportion to the steps downward from the top by which grace is mediated," writes René Roques, "purification, illumination, and perfection lose their force and brilliance."[6] Contrary to the writings of Plotinus, Iamblichus, or the latter's teacher, Proclus, this procession down the scale is no natural expansion of the One outside itself, an effusion of being or divine radiance. Its *proodos* is diacritical, and this *diakrisis* is truly critical in the sense that each level of mediation, by reason of the gratuitousness of divine gifts, reenacts Revelation anew. What Daniel Bougnoux calls the world's "mediatic impasto"—its thickening, by multiplication of ladders and rungs—is a prominent feature of spiritual "thickness" as well. If, in the Greek language, "diabolical" is that which divides, while "symbolic" (*sumballein*) is that which unites, there are grounds for claiming that *the transmission of the divine is structured diabolically*. *Diablos*, properly speaking "he who puts himself across," in the sense of "athwart, in the way or across the course of," is the alias or alter ego of *angelos*, the messenger. A disconcerting reversibility of order into disorder. To synthesize, the devil is not necessarily God's other; he can be God exercising his power. The noise is in the message itself.

MEDIABOLICS

For these reasons, *mediology* in Roman Catholic code might just as easily call itself "demonology" as "angelology." And here is a third lesson: at every instant the angel can reverse his role into demon, the vector *toward* form a screen *between*, the channel obstruct. At the core of each Messiah (and not next to or against him) slumbers an Antichrist. The demon leader of the deposed rebel angels had been the most exalted of the angelic spirits, for the more closely an angel approaches God the more tempted he will be to wish to resemble God. "From the greatest height fallen, he is the one who lowest falls": the Tarpeian Rock is close to the Capitol. Whether one takes the angel for God or the vector for the message, both reflect the satanic side of communication societies brought out so ingeniously by Michel Serres.[7] Our news carriers and bearers no longer know how to step aside. Lacan steps onto the psychoanalytic stage as Freud's angel; eventually one no longer consults Freud but cites Lacan. We no longer go to the theater to see a play by Shakespeare, we go to see a Lavaudant or a Chéreau. We no longer listen to Bach's records but Glenn Gould's. Or we read a book only through the interview with the author interpreting it himself for us in the newspaper. There are traffic jams on this highway. Mediators no longer turn out to be those delicate feathered cherubs who flutter away once the message is delivered, like Gabriel having made the Annunciation to Mary. These prideful presences take themselves for the message itself. A profane version of the angels' fall, mediatic bottlenecks take place when the announcer promotes himself by public display or the official voice, instrument, or organ rebels against its designated function. "All power to the transmitters!" The vehicles take the passenger's place, meaning's place, transporting only themselves. The event's announcement stands in for it.

Traveling backward from the perverse effect of message-delivery systems to its cause, I will thus state, "What renders the message possible also makes probable its perversion." Or, in more critical parlance, the optimal enabling conditions for successful handling of a message are those equally for its misappropriation. Such ambivalence is hard to take. Here was the angel, there to protect us from the demonic. What becomes of salvation if angel proves to be demon? The risk indeed inheres in the function, and Christian theology clearly saw this. In opposition to dualism of the Iranian, Essenian, or Catharist strains, Christianity denied itself the Manichaean facility with which Evil was accorded independent substantiality. Every medium is the best and the worst of things. Aesop made a proverb of this repeated every day, yet is there any more vexing mystery, at bottom, than good's convertibility to evil? Satan is still an *angel*, however fallen and rebellious. Saint George endlessly switches places with the dragon; of nothing can we be certain, and least of all of his shadow. Evil, Good have the same origin. Dream on, ye who would abandon thyself to the one without taking a taste of the other. The only way through, via the channel, implies blockage by it, being *in* the way. No one can at once want to be *understood* and avoid being *stood under* some misunderstanding. Not the one without the other. The Book of Henoch ascribes to apostate angels the double role of civilizers and corrupters. Reaching earth they bring the sword with the plow, flirtation with love. From the first morn ambiguity was present, along with disappointment.

"A very powerful spirit, Socrates, and spirits, you know, are halfway between god and man," says Diotima in *The Symposium*.[8] The medial role of the Hellenic demon was already, as early as Hesiod, that of the Christian angel: "They are the envoys and interpreters that ply between heaven and earth, flying upward with our worship and our prayers, and descending with the heavenly answers and commandments, and since they are between the two estates they weld both sides together and merge them into one great whole" (p. 555, 202e). Elsewhere, in the *Epinomis* (984e), Plato situates demons, within the hierarchy of elements, at the level of air, the intermediary between heaven and earth. Starting out, the *daimon*, Socrates' guardian angel and his special adviser, is beneficent and good. But associated as he was with the world of oracles, magic, and other divinatory practices, he could not evade for long a baleful conversion. One encounters the lustrous emissary taking on darkness too in the course of the exegeses (Xenocrates, Plutarch, and Iamblichus all lay emphasis, after Plato, on maleficent demons). Christian dogma stipulates that the demons were created by God, however indirectly, and that they were created good and exert a certain dominance over humanity with divine permission. In the words of the book of Revelation, a third of the demons were created—by nature and in the form of—angels, this percentage taking the first polling of the prideful ones in the troop. They use the same means as angels: suggestive, erotic, and carnal. They act on the body by the body, which is more vulnerable than the soul to impure temptations. The demon, said Theresa of Avila, can influence the soul only by the body and the faculties of sense, by imagination, sensitivity, memory, and the lower faculties. Initially soul and body are indistinguishable. Woman interposes as well between man and Satan, when she is named Eve, as she does between man and God, when named Mary. Remarking the cruel hesitation between extremes, Baudelaire sounded a warning by insisting that the devil's most alluring ruse is persuading us he does not exist. How? By borrowing the angels' smile. A clever sinner, he who knows how to recognize at a glance good and evil, how to distinguish savior from bringer of death. Would there still be tales of love and war if human beings did not of necessity, in the beginning of the relation, take one for the other?

What exactly, in sum, can one read in the angels? Of what do they serve as legend? Is it admonition or premonition?

They weld an sos to human finitude. Distress and dereliction. Immediacy has disappeared, along with paradise, so that we are delivered over to uncontrollable intermediaries, multiplying the ladder's rungs even as we climb toward the ultimate end. We must pass through a succession of interconnecting porticoes, corridors, and stairways; a maze of reflections more or less misleading, interpreters more or less trustworthy, interlocutors more or less dubious. And what we take as a vestibule is the dwelling place itself: the centrality of the hallway. The angel is the grimace of an absent God, the small change left over from a disappearing act. A Sisyphus with wings recurs throughout sacred history. One can see in it an insistent sign of our incompleteness, of the adult's unreadiness to climb out of childhood, and of history's to put prehistory behind it. The master will always be needed to learn to get by without a master, and a wing always needed to reach lofty heights. One cannot manage all by oneself. Gates do not open without gatekeepers. We cannot do without lookouts, guides, or protectors; without big brothers or sisters; without counselors of the psyche in its face-off with death. Or without front-rank men to file behind, presidents to represent the nation, presiding spirits to navigate us through.

Is the angel the herald of our subjection? Yes, this too-neglected fable whispers in our ear the involuntary moral that with assistance, infantilized and immature, we will cling to life. The confused rustle of these birds of the soul flitting, ambiguous, between the Eternal and us, let us hear in it, rather, the three knocks that signal the start of the play, a reminder of our essential infirmity: mediation will be our fate. Souls gain access to what is vital to them only through the intermediary of foreign incorporations. To put it in starkest terms: though it be our most cherished wish, it does not appear that we can ever become atheists in the sense the young Marx understands that prospect when he defines religion as recognizing Man through a detour, an intermediary (even recognizing oneself as an atheist through an atheistic state, he adds, is to remain religious). Wherever we, agnostics or believers, may go, an angel will await us on the doorstep. He will be a teacher, an escort, a priest of the abbey, or a guru, and it is futile to want to do without his intercession. The evidence shows that the immediacy of a relation to oneself, of which we as individuals or a community cannot stop dreaming, will never, ever, come about.

4

Fault Lines

Far from removing us from our own era's ugly side, this compulsory digression through the passageway embellished with angelic lore paradoxically flings open the door to life on the street. Such is the agency, at once meddlesome and necessary, of mediums. Better understanding our own present led to the detour of our atemporal salvific myths. We can read, like an open book, the sinner's destiny of expropriated selfhood, as illustrated by the code of Roman Catholicism, in line with our own actuality. The latest news stories make the common coinage of political, military, and indeed terroristic urgencies out of a metahistorical condition.

THE SEISMIC ZONE

The day no longer belonging to the artist-engineers of the Italian Renaissance, social and managerial circles devoted to technology and industry simply no longer mingle with circles of artists and intellectuals. Students in applied arts and vocational training seldom mingle with students in the liberal arts at the Ecole Normale: "to each his stock in trade." The role of go-between from one sphere of influence to another falls to the mediologist, a socially infelicitous position because it lacks affiliation with a preestablished group or professional body. This is someone who takes a properly philosophic interest in the history of technology and observes (as a student of technology) the life of forms and mind. This straddling of two cultures is no easier to live than it is to conceptualize. Our nonindigenous misfit nonetheless has a sneaking suspicion of being at the matter's heart. Isn't the awkwardness of this position, being in both places yet belonging fully to neither, typical of most people's along the century's continental divide? Two subterranean tectonic plates meet at the thrust fault of contemporary societies and overlap mysteriously: innovation and memory. Above them the tightrope walker strings taut a philosophic wire, seeking to discern both the effects on consciousness of material devices and devisings and the technological determinants of cultural mutations. The methodological wager makes an intelligible tally of signs within that zone of hyperresponsive frictions where one is forced to locate the epicenter of perceptible quakes. Their shock waves can be followed on television by everybody, from day to day.

The mediologist interprets our grand crisis of identity as the result of a confrontation between the technologic crust of the human species, its renewal ceaselessly accelerated, and the underground mantle of cultures, under violent compression as they meet despite the latter's weakened elasticity. Out of this comes a series of tremors of state that can be measured from one to nine on a mediologic Richter scale, with fissures, cracks, breccias, and catastrophes, on up to collapses of the first magnitude (Iran, Algeria, Afghanistan, etc.). In these areas mediology confines one to seismology. Can one not discover a premonition, in the battle between ethnic memory and the tendencies of a new technology, of what will be at stake in the next century? Put graphically, this is a question of God versus the silicon chip, and the struggle's outcome could well come down to a paradoxical reactivation of orthodoxy by computers. If so, the future would thus be given over to anachronisms (something not without its drawbacks for the time being). We are indeed witnessing a growing imbalance between territories and temporalities experienced as simultaneities: the rapidity of our evolutionary rhythm of assimilating knowledge is thrown off by the relative inertia of our various fealties and our sense of membership in, or obedience to, different associations, doctrines, or affiliations. Equally jarring, the more uniformly weightless our objects and networks become, the more enmeshed we seem to be in long-standing mythologies and attachments. The pace of our displacement intensifies the counterneed for placement. Cries of human protest are the understandable expression of those caught within the cultural equivalent of geologic unconformities. In every latitude, sufferings take different moral forms; still, the larger evolutionary rift seems identifiable everywhere, though generally viewed with pathos (instead of clear-sightedness) by moralists who diagnose the irreparable rupture of the twentieth century.

Remarks about the wide discrepancy between the age of death camps and the age of technocratically neutral labs, mainly *political* panic, and the inconvenience of *technological* takeover hardly seem original. But I will begin with the observation that this very real difference was not on the agenda of yesterday's messianists heralding a return to the past, whether those worshiping Machine or those worshiping Mind. If we are to survey the late twentieth century's gaping divide between Machine and Spirit, we must begin by conceding that the musical score written for the maker of tools does not exclusively apply to the instruments of a culture. The human animal survives by consulting his dreams as much as his prosthetic devices. Collectively deploying the latter, however, involves obeying different laws from those governing collective imaginings and symbolic aspirations and beliefs. Homo sapiens is in this sense an incoherent creature; what he takes in of instrumental reason does not ipso facto produce an equivalent quantum of human belief out the other end, notwithstanding the suppositions made by the Servan-Schreibers, Alvin Tofflers, and Bill Gateses of each recently heralded threshold of the new technological age.

Whoever refuses to grasp both ends of the thread carefully risks treating the problems by overlooking the problematics. At the one end, there are the engineers who just yesterday serenely prophesied the advent of the global village without foreseeing that the cloud surrounding the silver lining of electronic uniculture was an unfortunate secession of reflexes. McLuhan's utopia reduced our hopes and dreams to the story of our tools. From the shrinking of distances he deduced the happy amalgamation of cultural memories; this meant blurring the two orders of space (technology) and time (culture). It discounted the human dimension of fantasy, when clearly Homo sapiens generates enthusiasms no less than bodies and tools of knowledge, performing science and magic in a simultaneous pas de deux. Holding the thread's other end, the sociologists, undaunted, go about studying identities, patrimonies, territories, minorities, and cultural hybridization while bracketing macrosystems and small miracles that, from jumbo jets to parabolic antennae, have truly rearranged the very foundations of configured living spaces.

The two camps will look unfavorably on the amateur student of transmission's to and fro. Ambivalence is his lot, the "neither/nor" his fate. In the same breath his pronouncements will disappoint both those who serve the deus in machina (believers in the technological factor's omnipotence) and those who prognosticate man-as-subject (for whom tools are transcended by the human or inhuman ends they are put to). But technological efficiency is at once less serious than futurologists take it to be—disdainful as they are of the many secret continuities of culture—and more pervasive than permitted by metaphysicians superbly indifferent to material life. It is possible to demonstrate at one and the same time that the steam engine, penicillin, and digital computing have both changed nothing and transformed everything. As far as the human condition goes, a brief for the one or the other can be entered; it is just a matter of choosing the scale and level of analysis. Consider what can be called the collective technologies of belief manufacture or belief propagation, the ones that condition so subtly and all-powerfully our different credulities via their particular circumstantialities, their channeling through certain senses, and so on (such as passage of information by word of mouth, public reading, private reading, radio and video, and the like). These still do not modify the basic anthropological need to believe, any more than the technologies of knowledge acquisition alter our competence and appetite for knowing. And yet it is true that a television-watching citizen will not give credence to the same values or types of personality as will a reader of written arguments or a listener to oral accounts. Changing from one physical medium to another modifies the regimens of belief and group affiliation. It is a sure thing that one does not put on a new culture the way one changes software or cars. No less sure is the fact that each period's cognitive systems are constructed as a function of the available technologies of intelligence, given that intelligence is not something enclosed within the individual's brain (Pierre Lévy). The wager consists, as it always does, in thinking and living with contradictory ideas.

In their generosity, the technophilic developers bank on the fact that, all things considered, collective identity is neither a finite and homogeneous entity nor the unique determinant of personal identity. Individuals are composed of layers, like a building of several floors (social class, language, nationality, region, profession, religion, sex, etc.). Ergo, runs the reasoning, why shouldn't the human race be similarly constructed in a divergent multiplicity of tiers? Hallelujahs will then be sung to the happy babelization of the earth as motherland transcending fatherland and to multicultural societies harmoniously juxtaposed and founded on a plurality of attachments, a source of richness, dialogue, and exchange. One quickly grasps why UNESCO, the literary-cultural supplements of our national weeklies, and international conferences should all rush to buy into this. Rhetorical excess aside, if the dialogue of cultures much vaunted by our discourses so often in fact resembles the same culture shock about which we read along the fissured surface of our interethnic squabbles and incivilities, can it not be ascribed to those gratings between geologic strata—technics and culture—each sliding in its opposite direction? For Tzvetan Todorov the *inter*cultural is constitutive of the cultural.[1] If this is true, no less does the leveling hybridization of lived worlds, with its phenomena of cross-acculturation and assimilation, seem itself to be embedded in a larger field of mediological interactions. There, the moorings beneath pull against the shimmering panoplies above, and our ethnic automatisms interact with our universal machines.

INTERDEPENDENCIES

It goes without saying that the field is complex. One speaks more appropriately of interactions and bipolarity than of entrenched antinomy. Bruno Latour and others have shown there is no discrete technological object purely technological and totally inhuman or reducible to a purely instrumental neutrality. Technology is freighted with positive or negative values, fitted into institutions or social networks (like the speed bump or the alarm clock). We would never understand that things can speak to us about human beings if inanimate objects were not endowed with a kind of social soul. The manufactured and even standardized machine-object (the automobile) can also vehiculate dreams, style, values, and the self-image of an era. Thus can it also materially emblematize an era's spirit in symbols, especially at a distance (think of the Deux Chevaux or the Mercedes). I will venture further to say that, even well before the culture industries came about, never has there been culture without machinery or the invention of a machine without a culture farther back in time. The technological gesture itself appears out of a laying of memory traces, the way an apprentice must go through certain motions, recorded and repeated and appropriated so as to be carried on. From gesture also the tool derives its efficacy, for which as much savoir-faire is needed to preserve the tradition mentally as caloric energy to enact it bodily. After the studies of Alain Gras and Philippe Breton, among others, we know just how much the history of mentalities fuses with that of our machines and how much that of our machines prolongs existing myths and nourishes new ones. This happened with Icarus, the Golem, Pygmalion, or Frankenstein. No stark demarcations can be traced between these domains, or sworn enemies drawn into contrived face-offs. Everybody has some firsthand idea of how much artisanal competence in handling certain materials or apparatus is assumed in the most minimal implementation of a cultural activity or conservation of documentary material, news, or other datum within a text, picture, or score. Recording, saving, archiving, and consulting: all imply know-how, sometimes personalized and sometimes, as so often today, delegated to machines.

As soon as one cuts through complication by filing under *culture* relations between people and under *technology* people's relations to things it
becomes clear that subject-subject relations are mediated by the objectively
material, as subject-object relations are mediated by subjectivities that are
underlying, collegial, or collective. Mediation works its will in both directions. This explains the perils of erecting Technology as an autonomous
megasubject, whether to demonize it as a megamachine, in the case of the
visionary technophobes, or to idolize it as the Good Mother, in the case of
cyberutopian delusionaries. A technologic determinism has the drawback
of cultivating only mechanistic causalities. The best cure for them is, yet
again, the history of technologies themselves, for which a simplified dia-
grammatic causality is ordinarily replaced by systemic tautological circles of
the type, say, that blames the lack of vegetation in the desert for inhibiting
rainfall there and the absence of rainfall for eliminating vegetation.

Invention proposes; community disposes. Each of these two agencies
holds "half the program" (in Daniel Bougnoux's phrase). If one denotes by
culture the system of practices, codes, rules, and expectations appertaining to
a historically constituted group—the national mindset—such a group con-
figures a sort of domestic interior that will be capable, as a function of its
needs, of either assimilating or rejecting a given innovation. Some specific
characteristics of a technology it will find useful in one situation, for some
purposes, others unusable (at least at first) in another situation. Much as each
organism selectively picks up from its environment pertinent information
that blinks its signals only to it, a lineage of cultural evolution singles out,
from a complex of available innovations, the ones most meaningful to it and
that it alone can best optimize. Nobody hypothesizes that Gutenberg's invention, introduced into New Guinea, would have produced the Renaissance or
that the Internet can make interactive cybernauts appear at the foot of moun-
tains in Nepal. And although nineteenth-century England possessed the
technological base for it (ranging from industrialized printing to railroads to
the educational network, scholarly grapevines, and institutional niches for
men of letters), it did not produce that culturally specific figure of the intellectual (typically French because historically overdetermined).

I find convincing those cultural historians such as Roger Chartier who
counter the theme of explosive technologic revolution with that of attitudi-
nal gradualism. They exhibit the ways in which changes in behavior in the
West preceded and anticipated the abrupt caesurae presumed to have pro-
voked or ushered in those changes. Revolutions in the practice of reading,
for example, fail to coincide perfectly with those of book production. As

early as the fourteenth century, Petrarch's humanistic writing inaugurated, at a time when copyists were still laboring in scriptoria, the tools and methods of easy readability it would take two centuries for printers to reinvent in the sixteenth. And the university system of the so-called *peciae*, or quires of exemplaria for student use, vastly expanded the production of manuscript texts two centuries before the advent of printing presses.[2] At the same moment in northern Europe, the *devotio moderna* was already entreating the faithful to read the Bible individually, well before Luther and Calvin. And the birth of the protobook, or codex, in the first century A.D.—well before Gutenberg obviously—precociously transferred graphic spaces from scrolled surface to portable volume, simultaneously enabling silent reading, marginal annotation, pagination, and new classifications first based on titles and then on authorship.

Need one truly choose between technicism and culturalism? What appears to make a revolution, such as that of printed texts in accounts such as Elizabeth Eisenstein's, is an encounter between an emergent disposition to praxis (method of reading, writing, classifying) and an innovational system of tools and media. Without the quasi-chromosomal conjunction of cultural breeding ground with new technology, an innovation will not come forward and take over.

DEMARCATION

Uses of the terms *technology* and *technics* are as numerous and contradictory as those of *culture*, so it is no easy task to grasp their proper meaning or what essentially separates them. Up to a relatively late stage in human evolutionary development, there was good reason to assimilate both technological and cultural instances under the category *art*, which, following its original definition, referred simply to that which contrasts with nature and its gifts (*ars est homo additus naturae*). The one and the other make up what is supernumerary: collective derivative productions, supplements to our genetic baggage, and learnings acquired from history rather than hereditary gifts. Past this common point, however, there is grave divergence in the series.

Let us cast a glance on our environs. In whichever country you visit at the end of this century you will, always and everywhere, find internal combustion engines, towers with power lines, airports, and computer terminals. And whether in Beijing, Cape Town, or Lima you will see the same objects, dress and brand names and countries of manufacture differing little from place to place. This is why, from one meridian to the other, you will feel comfortable and seldom out of your element or exiled, because human beings in 1999 share the same standardized competencies. How to use a car, keyboard, or escalator will not change according to latitude and social milieu. You may well be caught terribly off guard, however, by Chinese characters and deftly handled chopsticks in Beijing, by the smooth sway of worshipers gospel-singing at mass in Cape Town, or by an Indian's shaking his head up and down for "no" in Lima. Had you been visiting Peking, Cape Town, or Lima in 1857 you might well not have come across a single one of those banal, unprestigious innovations you had become so used to in Europe (so much so as to have missed their artifactual character). But then as now you would have come up against the same ideograms, cuisine, and set of gestures and experienced similar moments of foreignness.

All of this puts us on the trail of a further distinction worth noting. Let us, again, designate *culture* from an anthropological viewpoint as the repertory of forms, intuitive schemas, and corporealized memories every society makes available to its members. Those cultural practices present *weak variability over time* and *strong diversity over space*. Conversely, technological realities register *strong variability over time* (in particular, from the period of the first industrial revolution) and *consistent uniformity over space*.[3] The dissymmetry between properties results in an almost perfect chiasmus. There are some three thousand spoken languages in the world and only three gauges for railroad track, two standard voltages for the world's appliances, and one International Civil Aviation Organization stipulating telecommunication among all airships in one code, English. But the intensive and persistent use of the French language would enable a resurrected Racine to converse as an equal with Claude Simon. A *technical system* translates coherences that for every age are woven among the different tools and apparatuses, at all points in the space of practice. A *cultural system* ensures, for one given locality and only one, those coherences that are knitted between periods and generations.

A contrast in rates of change, between the evolutionary stability of civilization's "geology" (or spheres of activity), on the one hand, and industrial innovation's fast-forwarding, on the other, induces the cultural equivalent of disturbed personality: a crisis of temporality. More than just discrepant rhythms of growth, these two time lines at variance with one another mark two wholly dissimilar regions of being. Our machines become dated like our sports records; not so our dreams or our poems. Human beings, who evade time through fantasy, plunge back into it through technology. Our *objects* hold fast to their historical context while our *works* can escape from them. These two orders of creation have a complicated history, certainly, but the history of technological objects arrows forward and is by nature perfectible. Successive technical variations of models and prototypes are arranged in relation to a quantifiable, increasing performance scale. They always go from a less to a more, as with speed or reliability; from a least to a better or best, as in efficiency, performance, and output; from a larger to a smaller, as with compactness; and so forth. In contrast, the history of civilizations aligns incommensurable totalities. Cultural relativism is conceivable—no culture legitimately being able to put itself forward as the standard for all the others—whereas technological relativism would hardly make sense, except aesthetically or speculatively. A tractor will outperform a plow, period. These things are not open for discussion as tastes and colors are. A balance sheet of yield per acre speaks for itself. For the descriptive ethnologist, no one group of people is superior to the others; for the historian of technology, or the technologist, some tools are indeed superior to others. In the cultural realm, before and after count for nothing; chronology is never an argument for or against.

Which things exactly, then, are technological, and which cultural? I suggest that *technologic* covers those devices or systems that, so to speak, carry a one-way ticket, and *cultural* those that are open to trips back in time at any moment in history. Once artillery was invented, no army sought to supply itself with crossbows. After the appearance of the railroad, no transportation authority made use of the stagecoach. After antibiotics, boiled decoctions changed their status. But in, say, art history, no irreversible ratcheting ever upward exists: Picasso can recycle *art nègre* for his own purposes, and I am permitted the luxury of preferring Cimabue to Dubuffet. All periods and all schools are fair game; cultural history does not obey time's arrow. And nothing warrants the supposition that Rawls is a more pertinent political philosopher than Rousseau just because he was born later or that the good Doctor Schweitzer had loftier ethics than Saint Vincent de Paul because he had stored up three additional centuries of spiritual experiences. In the history of forms, norms, and values, the notion of an irreversible threshold or watershed lacks pertinence. Yesterday's technological object informs me about the one I had in my hands yesterday. Yesterday's preserved painting or myth teaches me about what I am today and can become tomorrow.

Information about our technological past is of very clear interest of course, but of a different nature, as demonstrated by its cultural afterlife. The industrial object that has fallen into disuse will be stored in an open-air museum of science and technology. The art object ends up in a museum *tout court*. No engineer will go off to the museum of technology maintained by the engineering institute in order to improve his present-day work, yet Cézanne regularly looked at Poussins in the Louvre to learn how to paint better: paradoxically, the work removed from its context continues to function, whereas the desituated machine is kaput. An art museum can be a school for apprentices, while a technology museum remains a storehouse of interesting dead curiosities. A museum of modern art in the hands of the active artist functions like a laboratory. A museum of industrial arts and sciences, as far as the active engineer is concerned, connotes only melancholy. Such is the unjust role switching of the archives. In a confrontation with the works that preceded it, the art object transmits futurity. The once-revolutionary industrial object, however, once it is withdrawn from circulation, transmits only pastness. Those who dismiss the philosopher's method of the *distinguo* as idle diversion will recall that in a sense not keeping the political and technologic orders separate has cost our species over the last two centuries a few hundred million souls. Were not the illusions of linear progress or progress as a mechanical certitude toward the end of the eighteenth century and the beginning of the industrial revolution the fruits of an excessive extrapolation of technoeconomical time onto politicocultural time? This conceptual confusion has engendered hopes without an object and thus in the end, at the point where we now find ourselves, a kind of groundless depression.

Let me put the same idea in other words. Culture is inherited; technology, received. Culture is transmitted by deliberate acts. It is a singular content of intimate concern to me, to my identity proper, for which I am personally responsible, it being incumbent on me to will it to those who will come after. Technology is transferred and disbursed spontaneously: I derive good from it but am not really needed by it; it stands in availability. (This points up the difference between conserved things and stocked items.) There are technological lineages but only *cultural* legacies. For those things that differentiate me from others, that single me out as different, I feel a sense of responsibility. Of those things by which we all resemble one another, I am a consumer, a user, a receiver, and a victim but not a designated recipient or beneficiary. For all its rendering possible and easy the act of messaging, technology is never itself a message. Only culture can be addressed to someone.

5

Tool Lines

It would require the prehistorian's detachment to put the daily news in proper perspective. In that light I see no reason why our contemporary disorders and excesses should obey other laws than those that have always obtained, since the earliest stages of social interaction. The paleontologist and material anthropologist André Leroi-Gourhan notes that cultural diversification has been the principal regulator of evolution at the level of Homo sapiens. This fact of observation must be admitted even by those who take to heart Auguste Comte's motto "The human species as one people." The unit of animal grouping turns out to be the species, and that of human consolidation the ethnic group or *ethnie*. In our particular zoological genus, Leroi-Gourhan argues, the ethnic group substitutes for the animal species, and human individuals are ethnically different, as are animals through speciation. There is of course no reason to draw from this, except in the case of racist pathology, the conclusion that to animal species' genetic isolation (tigers cannot mix with bears) correspond barriers between ethnic groups. All cultures are hybridizable, their traits exportable and their peoples mixable. It is no less the case, though, that symbolizing or representational practices (linked to a determinate language) give rise, and assume a sense of belonging, to the *ethnie*, or ethnic grouping, whereas technological practices put into play *universal* forms and determinisms. Hence the same phylogenetic lineages for tools are able to pass across boundaries between people who might otherwise have little contact with one another.

It is not by chance that two important moments seem to have coincided chronologically: (1) the appearance of the Neanderthals, sometime during the third (Riss-Würm) interglacial period of the Upper Pleistocene more than one hundred thousand years ago, during which appeared the first traces of abstract symbolism, of figural code; and (2) the beginnings of evidence for a diversification into ethnic groupings within the species of Homo sapiens. The mechanical memory (e.g., operative steps in a practice, familiarity with environment, and ritual repetitions) as well as conscious, creative memory (leaving carved or written traces whose remains have been found) both crystallize over the long run into an ethnic capital in which we may recognize a distinct collective personality, a family resemblance, the genius of a people, the flavor of a locality, or a *parfum d'enfance*. Such are the forms, perceptible to ear, eye, or nose, of a comfort in belonging that is unconscious and subjective. Anthropology conceptualizes it under *culture*, and it is obviously based in a language, the most tenacious of all group memories. All human beings have the same emotions but do not express them with their body in the same ways: their code is cultural (or ethnic). It would not be absurd to maintain, in opposition to the clichés, that culture is what splits apart the human species while technology unites them. The one causes them to dig in, with trenches and barricades; the other clears and flattens the way. Technological space is isotropic: innovation is diffused outward in all directions, which have in this respect the same physical properties. Cultural space can be called anisotropic, as is, to a superlative degree, religious space. With its organization based on a center radiating outward (Jerusalem, Rome, or Mecca), its sacramental sites (shrines), its extraurban peripheries (mission lands for proselytizing), and its hostile perimeters (infidels at the circumference), religious space is never all in one piece. A cultural system suggests a fanning outward of *places*. A technical system evokes a combination of *tracks*. (If words have any meaning, the coinage *cyberculture* is a contradiction in terms.) Drawing up an official registry of the present state of technological development would yield a picture of convergences. Were we to do the same for mentalities, we would have an inventory of differences.

If we remove from *ethnie* the unfortunate connotation given it by colonial anthropology (the noncivilized) and by political polemics (tribe versus nation), we replace the pair *technology/culture* with the opposition *technological convergence/ethnic divergence*, which would be its translation further developed. The convergence of technological inventions is due to the universality of nature's constraints and laws. For example, all rooftops, whatever their location, tend to adopt the form of two sloping sides, all axes the world over are equipped with handles, all boat hulls take the fusiform shape (Alain observed, "It is the sea that fashions boats, choosing those that are suited and destroying the others"[1]). True, some technologic systems have, for various cultural reasons, remained immobilized in certain civilizations such as the pre-Columbian Americas, the Muslim world, and China. But once they have appeared and made headway, the tools of each morphological lineage (choppers, bifaces, scrapers, pointed implements, blade, knife, etc.) increasingly resemble one another in every culture. Culture can endow the shield, fishhook, hoe, or typewriter with a singular decorative style; the *functional* formula will inexorably impose itself on all of them by dint of a mechanical determinism. *Material progress is not anchored in native soil.* It systematizes, equalizes, and homogenizes. Electromagnetic airspace erases national frontiers, as do Comsats. In this sense, the technological structuring of the world, taking us from wheel to airplane, also carries with it the very real potential to *culturally* destructure the world. Inventive dynamism rocks local and national attachments to their core; it bulldozes language barriers, communitarian proximities, and the exotic diversity of customs. Under the purely formal range of variation in design, identity of function reduces the many to the one: internal uniformity of the object, unity of the system of objects.

Individual devices and systems tend toward integral uniformity in their internal elements, just as the different technological lineages of such "individuals" tend toward larger integration. To make homologous, normalized, and standardized is the general tendency. The clock came historically to mark the same hour in the four corners of a country and then brought about standard Greenwich mean time and the planetwide system of twenty-four time zones. From country to country, the railroads adopted a standardized gauge. The electric telegraph, which enabled an extension of rail transport by helping resolve the problem of travel over the same railway, also produced—in Morse's alphabet—the first international code of signals (the technology of objects and that of signs mutually determine each other). Just yesterday, television produced transmission standards much as the TV decoder industry has established its own. Likewise do we now witness the digital encoding of all information so as to make all channels in the end converge through the phone line, integrating telecommunications, nationwide computer terminals, TV, movies, CDs, and pixellated photographs into *unimedia* (*multimedia* is a misnomer, the world having become techno-uniform). The concretization of the technological individual, or the growing integration of parts into a whole that is nevertheless strongly marked by individuation (an observation of Simondon's), governs, by ricochet effect on the large scale, the technicized world as a whole on its inexorable march toward perfection and completeness. The planet toward which we are heading, in other words, will be one complete, interconnected—or intracon-nected—whole, in which the interdependence of the elements will prevail over and soon frustrate any remaining values of originality. With the railway and airway networks ensuring the circulation of human beings all over the world, the banking networks that of capital, and the telecommunications networks that of signs, images, and sounds, the reticulate planet's space is at once turned into a desert and forged into a unity. Our technologic macrosystems of travel and communication—postal, aeronautic, electron-ic, telephonic, and so forth—become international by vocation and neces-sity. Cooperation among operating systems—interoperability—is the watchword of a universe of compatibles made smooth and reworked by the special exigencies of an imperious material implementation that made its first appearance in the nineteenth century and endows utopian formalism with a genuinely operational content called "system" or "network." To the coherence of its internal connections is added the voluntarism of its future-driven projections, such that this systemic deployment of resources and equipment naturally sets its sights on the totalitarian or totalizing. We knew this goal as national in the last century, know it now as global, and will know it as intergalactic one day.[2] A planet-city, woven together into the web of a system of systems, was the Saint-Simonian utopia, with its ideal of impris-oning the globe in order to liberate men. It is hardly surprising that as tech-nologies become more complex, the world in a sense becomes simpler or simpler-minded, as its irregularities and harlequinesque miscellany are reduced to the lowest common denominator.

What place does the process of indifferentiation imposed by the techno-logic empire cede to remaining pockets of ethnic singularities? Implacably linear logic tells us it is minimal or residual. Buddhism is not interoperable with Christianity, nor the latter with Shiism. When macrosystems are global-ized, what kind of survival is allotted the familiar contacts and various reser-voirs of difference strewn here and there that balk all norms of equal access? The answer is none, if indeed the ultima ratio of human history turns out to be the Darwinian dynamism of technological progress (natural selection of the best through elimination of the least efficient). And if managerial reason governs all like an autocracy, no places will be left save a few government-funded Indian reservations, some vacationers' hinterlands, and a couple of pleasant and costly open-air museums in the center of each megalopolis. Did not Leroi-Gourhan himself proclaim the obsolescence of the ethnic structur-ing of human groups and the advent of a planetary mega-*ethnos*?

The facts for once do not seem to put him in the right, and it is here that this Collège de France professor and I diverge. The world one can call synthesized *technologically* has not become unified *ethnically*. So little progress has it made in this direction that political chroniclers from now on will have to remake themselves into ethnographers.[3] The widespread nomadism of objects tending toward a single currency has not produced a comparably ubiquitous nomadic subject. Culture's answer to the imperative uniformization of the species' technoeconomic surroundings has been, defying all expectations, an imperious politicoethnic Balkanization. Taking into account François Dagognet's formulation that matter travels faster than mind,[4] one could understand this discrepancy as a desynchronization of, or difference in, rates, the simple effect of inertia from culture's relative slowness of change. We should then expect that technology's transdivisional megamachine will swallow whole the minimemories of folklore. In prosaic allegory, the universal McDonalds (our megaethnic fast food) will end up permanently shutting the doors of Thai, Chinese, Indian, and Moroccan restaurants in London, New York, and Paris. This example will bring a smile to the faces of those who could care less about the culinary arts. But let us read, rather, in this fanciful blow to gustatory sensibilities, the facetious counterpart to a deconcerting phenomenon. This latter is a tough fishbone to swallow and consists of a negative retroactive effect of technology on culture. We can sum it up with the sobriquet "the jogging effect of technological progress."

RETROGRADE PROGRESS

In the 1950s certain futurists were predicting with confidence that city dwellers' immoderate use of the automobile would soon cause their lower extremities to atrophy as bipeds on motorized wheels grew more and more unaccustomed to walking. What did we see instead? This: ever since urbanites no longer walk they have ended up . . . running. And with fanatic devotion. In parks or, lacking that, in the living room, on treadmills.

The Jogging Effect in the Archive

In the technicist worldview, which diminishes memory to its documentary function, constructing gigantic libraries in the form of mastabas, towers, or palaces is a rather pathetic absurdity. In our day of delocalized on-line access and long-distance digital consultation, electronic circulation should for all intents and purposes render the concentration of materials in physical sites useless. But in fact the centrifugal dematerialization of data's supporting base increases our collective need to recenter ourselves on the basis of symbolic reference points. "The more eclectic the content," argues Michel Melot, "the more homogeneous the container."[5] The less there is of collective coherence, the greater the number of communitarian symbols, that is, ostensible mediations that knit the individual to a collective heritage whose stability and visibility are reassuring. Hence the proliferation of museums (of which it has been estimated that an average of one opens somewhere in the world every day). And hence the construction, not only in the old European capital cities (Paris, London) but also by younger nations the most divested of resources and archives, of lavish and monumental national libraries at such places as Tallin, Odessa, Algiers, or Niamcy. These technologically superfluous extravagances are yet deemed necessary *ethnically*. Rather than erasing sites of memory and commemoration, digital delocalization and audiovisual amnesia generate them in profusion. The spirits of marble are revived by the flux around them.

The Jogging Effect in Space

Video on demand and video cameras that broadcast live pictures of specific geographic sites, night and day, over the Internet should, one would think, favor armchair travel. Cannot one now hop over continents while staying at home, just by connecting to a server? The Internaut need not depart to arrive. Panoptical inertia should reign. How do things in fact stand, however? In the same manner that the electronic reproduction of documents, readable only in light onscreen, has also augmented their reproduction *on paper*, the more frequent the long-distance transmissions the more numerous the instances of physical transportation. Telecommunications have contributed to making tourism the largest industry in the world. The real surprise is that, as we shrink distances, we are all the more compelled to explore the periphery. The national highways have repopulated the hiking trails. Human feet created the love of the land; the horse, the nation; automobiles, the continent; planes, the planet; rockets, the cosmos. The hewing of the land in conformity with the needs of successive transportation systems reminds us that the most natural space of landscape has a technological history.[6] We can take some comfort in the fact that each novel form of vehiculation, far from wiping out the previous territory, tends to give it a new value. What the land loses in functional value, it can soon recoup in affective flavor. The small scale of which new macroeconomies dispossess us is appropriated by culture, to be set up as a touchstone and a new foundation. Since going to the moon, we have been relearning a certain love of the land. It is not the least of charms proper to the interlocked, tangled space in which we now move that technological progress exhibits the virtue of craftily undoing, with each revolution in locomotion, the catastrophes it is expected to precipitate. Potentially we can all feather our nests if we are wired into the new terrestrial ecosystem. The more vast distances are domesticated, the more small is beautiful.

The Jogging Effect in Languages

Global linguistic anglicization, many thought, should have proven linguici-dal for French and other national tongues. It has not happened that way. The language of the sciences, the stock markets, and other networks is reawakening the linguistic patriotism of those subject to domination, and this suggests rather the necessity of plurilinguism. The culture/technology dialectic, which in this case means the tension between maternal speech and the vehicular lingua franca, makes multinational unilinguism (i.e., English as the language of a united Europe)—certainly an economic ideal of the entrepreneurs in federations—into a dream that is functional but nonviable in the souls of distinct peoples and their traditions. Obligatory courses in English in secondary school and Americanized modes of usage, signs, and scientific reviews revive the creative sap of creole languages and the combativeness of dialects, something that is especially true in Europe, with its some sixty imbricate spoken tongues. We had expected that normalization by stereotype would transform all these living idioms into dead languages, confining them nobly to the literary registry or degrading them into provincial patois more or less in a state of vagrancy. Yet in the face of the new utilitarian medium, the language of choice becomes one's native speech, territorial and useless.[7] The vernacular is resupplying itself with mythic value, becoming a site of spiritual, religious, or magical references. Hence the renaissance of Hebrew and classical Arabic, once almost thought to be dead, and of Corsican, Breton, Gaelic, Flemish, Basque, and so on. Pan-national affiliations founded on a communal idiom make their appearance in diplomacy, with Francophonic and the Hispanophonic countries. Refusing to die, living languages reterritorialize the producer-consumers. Culture is on the side of the vital principle, whose nature is to be multiple, disruptive, and proliferous—the opposite of technology, if you prefer.

The Jogging Effect in Clothing

The way peoples dress is a distinctive mark of our social zoology, and we have seen how human living practices are distributed by ethnic units. Dress too, as much as language, is a typical feature of ethnicity: Leroi-Gourhan rightly detected in "the loss of national and professional attire the most striking sign of ethnic disintegration."[8] Sartorial uniformity signals a new interchangeability among individuals not dissimilar to technology in that it divests them of their national, regional, or professional collective personality (as members of the armed forces, the bar, the clergy, the university, and so on). Blue jeans, T-shirt, jacket—clothing's lowest common denominator, imitated from the strongest U.S. model of identification—is offset by fashion, tattooing, and piercing, as well as a debauchery of coifs and costumes, through images on film screens or ludic delegation. We behold the success of sight-and-sound historical reenactments in situ (of the Puy-du-Fou variety reconstructing in colorful detail the royalist revolt of the Vendée), movie and TV productions with their period costumes, and countless civic or regional pageants in ceremonial and local garb.

But enough listing of interminable symptoms. Are all these secondary compensations manifestations of recoil or of chain reaction? Are they futureless irredentisms, or are they homogeneity's generalized exacerbation of the endogenous? I lean toward the latter. Why not understand the struggle for cultural exceptionalism (to the iron law of technologic homogeneity) as a burst of biodiversity and in this respect as a completely natural impulse? How can we decry its traditionalism or stigmatize it a priori as reactionary given that we can never know in advance exactly what is unleashed by ricochet when a particular ecosystem, with its highly specific flora and fauna, is destroyed somewhere in the backwaters of the environment? Our biosphere's living species took hundreds of millions of years to adapt and flourish and that of the noosphere's human cultures required thousands. Having both been sculpted by a complex sequence of selective operations, mutations, and recompositions, they are both exposed to higher and higher rates of extinction. Ecologists combat the destruction of the living genetic libraries that are plants and animals. How can our sensibilities similarly allow without protest the extinction of the cultural *mnemothecas* [*Pinacothecas* (from Greek *pinax, pinakos,* "picture," and *thēke,* "repository")* were the ancient world's picture galleries. Debray has coined his term for memory galleries along similar lines.—Trans.] that have been produced by the creative evolution of forms and signs? Why should the disappearance of national traditions of cinema, or minority literatures, or languishing arts and crafts not stir up the same worry that has focused on the extermination of whales and seals? Technologic man's needs extend, and for the same reason, to nature as much as culture, to national parks, gardening, birdsong, and squirrels in town squares as much as to spectacles and dramatizations, incomprehensible ancient myths, and conjurers' books. In too high dosages, technicity throws off kilter the civilized organisms (greater metropolitan areas with their suburbias). Having passed beyond a certain stage of denaturation, civilization refashions nature technologically, in a made-to-measure manner. Gaia is mixed into virtual nature on CD-ROM, with tides and thunder and robin redbreast, in order not to succumb to the toxic overhumanization of our transistorized, fiber-optically cabled, air-conditioned, video-surveilled surroundings. So much, thus, does the human still crave, in order to breathe, nonhuman spaces. And just as living beings who are too well equipped require a modicum of cosmos, so our cosmic integration requires a modicum of ethnicity. Still, this bottom-line preservation of differences has its risks: returning to balance can itself become convulsive.

This is the case when the identity spasm, as a reflex against the utilitarian eradication of peripheral memories, pushes one to the point of fundamentalist insurrection. Idiosyncrasy's revenge against uniformity (of which God's revenge appears as an exasperated variant in places most convulsively ravaged by industry) is computer engineering's unanticipated unhappy surprise, much as territoriality remains the bugaboo of free-market dogma. The lost tacit agreements are recouped in the exaggerations of autochthony, the nervous reflex of group belonging, and other returns of all that the ideal of global Man repressed. The boomerang strikes at the very heart of the postindustrial. It is precisely in those richest Western countries where urban centers, political parties, churches, television stations, buildings and roads, houses and stores, and tastes and odors are the most interchangeable (or the least identifiable) that cultural singularities are most insisted on and valued. Technologically homogeneous decor, a diminution of local color toward the worldwide zero—its "somewhere, anywhere" look—simultaneously throws the internal heterogeneity of the United States into high relief, pushing people into persnickety respect for difference. A highly standardized circle of identical experiences and references, associated with television's amputation of historical memory, puts the notorious "gap" question frequently on the agenda: gender gap or ethnic gap. This exacerbated cult of minority sensibilities is what comes under ridicule as political correctness, with its officiation of and censoriousness toward appellations potentially offensive to each racial, sexual, or religious group. Monotechnological impoverishment exalts multicultural advocacies. And the depoliticization of lived experience exorbitantly repoliticizes the universe of symbols (right up to the preciosity in prescribed periphrases). This is proof from within the workings of a country that prides itself on being a beacon that one cannot regularize on the far side without balkanizing on the near.

A supplementary example is worldwide sports. The caricaturish national ethnocentrism that characterizes the retransmission of the televised Olympic Games—the ninety-odd participating countries shamelessly patriotizing the competition by focusing exclusively on their own medal winning—demonstrates how payment in full is really made for the "great universal celebration." Each telespectating public beholds not the whole but its own share of this muscular parody of Comte's Religion of Humanity, the cross-border religion of returns on investment in body capital. From the opening camera shots, its electronic high mass is instantaneously framed for national consumption. It is as though the globalization of objects and signs bore as its obverse the tribalization of subjects and values.

One would thus be wrong to see in the planet-city's birth a bid for universal cosmopolitanism. The ratio of one inhabitant out of ten living in a city in the world of 1900 has changed today to one out of two. But the transformation of the old walled cities into open and indistinct agglomerations gives rise to a savage ruralization of mentalities. The Arab-Islamic world has seen the numbers of its citizens increase fiftyfold in one century, and fundamentalist militancy has followed apace. The phenomenon represents a backlash in cities rather than the countryside, peculiar to shanty towns and overcrowded suburbs rather than traditional historical centers. It wakens rebellion especially among rural transplants who lose their bearings in the megalopolises, as well as among the scientists and technicians (rather than the literature students) in the universities. In the zones where tradition dictated life structured by faith, fundamentalism takes on the guise of a culture for those decultured by technology or a return to the soil for those uprooted from it. Generally it is the recent immigrants, migrants, and immigrés who preach a return to the sources. Whether we think of the Lubavitchers, or the charismatics, or "the bearded ones," messianic effervescence or the itch of orthodoxy often take hold of the excluded and deracinated first, leaving moderation and compromise to the old money of long duration and so-called good stock. Dogma and moral turmoil wrestle dialectically. It really seems, indeed, that history takes back with one hand what it grants with the other: openness here, closure there.

Crumbling ramparts of ancient animosities have been raised again into great walls; commemorative pedestals brutally uprighted crack the planisphere in a thousand places. Setting these divisions back in place has already helped dismantle the Soviet Union, tests the peace in Europe, threatens U.S. cohesion, and reawakens strife in Asia. Even if technology's addition to the equation may not necessarily correspond to a proportionate increase in barbarism, it must be conceded that the former has been shown to not hinder the latter. Nor has progress in industrial performance and commercial transactions worked against a regression of civilities and coexistences. An evolved nation-state can become tribal again, and a Republic of fellow citizens become a racialist consanguinity. When communitarian drives reach paradoxical high tide in the age of interdependencies, do we not witness, within the parliaments and governments of the most self-regulating representational democracies, a replacement, in parliament and government, by ethnocultural interest groups of the old ideologically cemented, dominant formations (witness politics in Israel, India, and Turkey)? The melting pots' mechanisms are grinding to a halt. A leveling of political differences may mean a renaissance in prepolitical identities—and, after deritualization, theocracy?

To escape the schizophrenia of a life enmeshed in networks that desynchronize and delocalize their users, is there no alternative to sliding back into the paranoia of pogroms and genocide? To trading in the mild insanity of technopolis for a furious insanity? No reasonable being will accept this price. We can still attempt to understand the intolerance we combat.

The rekindled vehemence of cultural differences, that ethnic vibrancy that turns bad, may be something like the panic syndrome of a timeless wisdom of communal bodies. For we know difference is not the opposite of harmony but its condition. (In René Girard's terms, where difference is in short supply, violence threatens.) An amorphous interculturalism's erasure of all demarcations among groups would be no less harmful for peace in the world of the future than is the intensification of those demarcations for peace in today's world. According to the "economic" hypothesis, the furor of nationalist and denominational independence movements in the post–cold war era translates an uncertain search, through experiments and errors, for a homeostatic equilibrium of ethnic groupings. Divided between the prospects of either cutting itself off from the world if it refuses to conform to majoritarian norms or drowning in the technocosm if it forgets its intragroup complicities, torn between its internal milieu (its cultural capital of habits and customs) and its eternal milieu (worldwide mechanistic capital), every developing ethnic microcosm would profit from a kind of automatic thermostat that would readjust the modernizing destabilization of its collective identity with an archaizing rebalancing of comparable intensity. We would then observe an alternation of phases of decentering and recentering, to correct one imbalance with another, however gropingly. In this way, each abrupt increase of progress and unification factors would provoke a no less qualitative elevation of regression and fragmentation factors. Thus would come about an autoregulatory reaffirmation of those collective personalities who so often behold their bubble burst under the onslaught of the smallest common operative convention of national and global life.[9] Is this speculative optimism or *amor fati*? We have already seen a metapsychology; in hommage to a great Viennese ancestor, may I immodestly venture a metamediology no less unverifiable and baroque? I am assessing the risks for the possible gain in seriousness of disciplinary reputation. It nonetheless remains true that whoever gives some thought to the strange attractions (of unity and struggle) that our tools and memories exert on one another will be tempted to conclude that, notwithstanding the low-valued scientific quality but at times epidemiological profitableness of these simplifications, postmodernity will be archaic if it is to be at all.

MAN'S PROPER STUDY

It appears that an untried label such as *mediology* does not always have its place on the shelf of shiniest novelties. Far from paying obeisance to futurist bigotries, it is a matter of asking why, at each instant, old and new never cease conversing and how so many abolished bibelots have managed to reach us. If mediology intends to come to grips with the processes, agents, and vectors that ensure thought's transmission, for all that it is not a novel frisson to classify furtively somewhere between the sociology of media and information and communication sciences, already venerable classifications. Aside from the fact that reflection about media has actually been around for several centuries—in the writings of illustrious thinkers and some lesser-known—its field of pertinence verges on prehistory and looks toward anthropology. At bottom, it examines what defines the human branch in its essence, by which means it can be distinguished from that of our simian

cousins, that is, Homo sapiens' aptitude for handing down acquired characters from one generation to the next, notwithstanding the most formal laws
of molecular biology. Does this not qualify, all things considered, as the
briefest and least inexact of definitions one might put forward of *culture*,
when one contrasts it with nature?

Outside of innate patterned response—types of imprinted behavior,
inscribed in their genetic codes—bears, badgers, or kites transmit nothing
tangible to their progeny. An animal's accumulated experience is lost for its
species as a whole. With each birth everything must begin afresh. It does
seem that chimps have the ability to transmit certain learned behaviors, all
connected with utilitarian functions, such as obtaining food or consolidating their ecological niche. The fact remains, however, we know of no animal
tradition that down through time can be superadded onto merely repeated
traits of the species. Primates learn one after the other; they do not accumulate knowledge in concert. Beyond that, excepting species drift and
genetic mutation (more on the geological scale), stable societies of the animal kingdom remain invariant. The polyandrous bee colony whose spright-
ly dance round the hive I observe today is the very same observed by Virgil
in the Roman countryside. But the group of Parisians I encounter turning a
corner in my neighborhood has different gestures and routines from inhab-
itants of the Seven Hills in the time of Augustus. Our family structures, for
instance, have evolved considerably, while throughout the ages the queen
bee is always fertilized by several males in the course of the same nuptial
flight. Here is to be found all the difference between natural life and historical life, the latter *an internalizing duration*: man is the only animal that can
conserve a trace of his grandfather and be modified by it. He invents himself insofar as he stores memory. Endowed with the same atomic structure,
subject to the same physical and biological laws as the other animal species,
and sharing the same planet, humankind is peculiar in that each of its members can undergo vicariously experiences he has not lived through personally. In Darwin's wake it was established that the experience acquired by an
individual—contrary to what Lamarck or Spencer had assumed—is not
preserved in the germinal plasma for passing on traits. Biology taught us
that the nucleic structure is not accessible to acquired experience and
remains invariable across the generations (François Jacob). What happened
to my ancestors has no record in the somatic cells of my embryo. Yet what I
am, what I believe, think, and choose, depends in large part on what their
works and days made them. Heredity belongs to all living beings; inheritance belongs only to man.

It was not lost upon the prescience of certain philosophical reflections that human difference was to be sought in this disconnect between the genetic and the nongenetic, well before positive knowledge made it possible to name and explain the logic of living being. In the first part of the *Second Discourse*, and with a premonitory intuition, Jean-Jacques Rousseau (in whom some see the founder of anthropology) considered this exceptional human trait to be of such a nature as to cut short controversies on the respective faculties of man and animal: strength, locomotion, sensibility, and so on. "But if the difficulties surrounding all these questions," he writes,

> should leave some room for dispute on this difference between man and animal, there is another very specific quality that distinguishes them and about which there can be no dispute: the faculty of self-per- fection, a faculty which, with the aid of circumstances, successfully develops all the others, and resides among us as much in the species as in the individual. By contrast an animal is at the end of a few months what it will be all its life; and its species is at the end of a thou- sand years what it was the first year of that thousand.[10]

This "very specific quality" had already inspired Pascal's grandiose vision of the human creature: "The entire sequence of men, over the course of so many centuries, must be considered as one and the same Man who subsists still, and who learns continuously."[11] A perspicacious Auguste Comte observed in his turn that humanity is made of many more of the dead than of the living and defined culture as the cult of the great deceased. The hymenopterous order to which bees belong is blissfully unaware of this eccentricity, and nobody thinks of the order of carnivores as mammals that are always growing and never ceasing to learn. A philanthropic worldview doing real damage to knowledge about man, the error of ancient philoso- phers who had indeed caught sight of the decisive importance of a genera- tive accumulation of transmittable symbols (the leap from transitory to cumulative), went astray in chiefly one way: by immediately tacking on to it moralizing considerations. Rather than examining this particularity back at its source upstream and exfoliating all its factual strangeness, they drowned it, so to speak, in the eschatological conclusions it suggested to them, with the result that on this matter speculation soon replaced genuine curiosity.

Let us therefore start by setting aside all values in order to distinguish operational knowledge from edification. Let us not be concerned with ask- ing, in the wake of our great philosophical ancestors, whether to this singu- lar faculty for archiving and circulating things not present at the beginning of the phylogenetic adventure there corresponds an improvement or decline of the phylum; whether it is better to see in it proof of perfectibility or corruptibility of the human being; whether it matters more to exalt culture, with Malraux, as the legacy of the world's nobility or to stigmatize it, with certain Nietzscheans, as marking the sick animal within us. The mediologist's more sober intention turns its back on these susceptibilities. He is satisfied with unfolding the full array of paraphernalia that can make an act of transmitting operate and with asking the question of method, "A legacy is made possible on what conditions?" It is a question as trivial as it is unwonted, as are all interesting questions whose habit is to make a banality into an enigma. That humans' evolution should obey hypothetical questions posed by Lamarck that had been discounted (concerning the inheritance of acquired characters) does not appear to trouble our spirits. The antinatural peculiarity could not seem more natural to everyone, especially as cultural transmission can be felt more in its effects, and is more crucial by reason of what is at stake, at the level of the species rather than the individual. We behave on this score like ungrateful heirs (some even make of that word an insult). And it is understandable why: the ancestral inheritance becomes corporeally absorbed into our behavior in the prereflexive and mechanically repetitive forms of cultural praxis (the postures of our bodies, the daily rhythms, the negotiations with our spatial environment). And it is also imposed on us in a materially objectivized form by our utensils, cities, routinized networks, and compendia of meaningful signs and symbols, that banal and quotidian habitat no obvious features of which any longer signal to us their artificiality. Both these gains—incorporated and objectified—are now virtually invisible to us. They are either blindingly obvious, when they are things, or they adhere to the retina from a very early age, when they are reflexes. There are reasons to excuse our nonchalance toward all that has preceded, equipped, and instructed us. Counted among them is the difficulty we have in mentally coordinating two timescales, each with its opposite coefficient. How is the individual whose nervous system alters and whose performances diminish with age (destroyed neurons not being replaced) to keep in mind spontaneously that the nervous system of humanity at large never ceases to multiply its connections and complicate its operations?

A naturalist was able to observe that we were the only species of animals capable of influencing its own evolution. What we are in fact is not something we are once and for all, because each day we add a new nonhereditary heritage to the genetic inheritance, one capable of retroacting on the latter, as can be seen with the engineering of life and genetic manipulations. The transference of coded information in the genes, ensured through the reproductive successions of organisms, goes forward, but along unnatural paths, and to the genetic program of life generally, human life superadds the technological prosthesis. "Life," remarks Georges Canguilhem, "always manages—without writing, well before writing and without any relation to writing—to do that which humanity has expressly sought through drawing, etching, writing, and printing, namely, to transmit messages."[12] Life embodies a chemical mnemonics, while culture puts forth a technologic mnemonics, a prolongation of the first one by other means. Culture's artificial resources make up a spring mechanism necessary to constituting a body of knowledge, as it is to producing a history; the agent of a process of becoming and the producer of learning both have need of these supplements to memory, added on to the biological baggage, of which the system of writing has been the most noteworthy. *Verba volant, scripta manent* (words fly away while letters remain). Does one not usually speak of a people without writing as lacking a history? The difference between human and natural history, Vico observed long ago, is that we made the first but not the second. Let us examine here the tools by which this difference comes about.

Reflection that leaves no trail, as Mallarmé noted, becomes evanescent. Geometry endures through Euclid's shapes; Christianity, through the Gospel's words; painting, through its lines and pigments. The trace, in its material insistence, transmutes the individual memory into social memory. To know is to remember, as the geometer slave recalls in Plato's *Meno*. The act of doing is no less so. Making the revolution, in part, means wanting to repeat past revolutions: one is a revolutionary out of conservatism. We have all read that "Men make history, but they do not make it just as they please; they do not make it under circumstances chosen by themselves, but under circumstances directly found, given and transmitted by the past." This "tradition of dead generations" that the author of *The Eighteenth Brumaire* portrayed as "weighing like a nightmare on the brain of the living" has since proven to be his takeoff runway, not only what tugs at us from behind but what carries the human race forward.[13] Everyone knows subversion can be the work of the best students, and with a devoted following the original worth of breaking with something goes up in smoke. A society that no longer recognizes distant ancestors shoots its own future in the foot.

Acts must not fade away with the lives of those who perform them, nor words with dying voices, and Euclid's postulates make their point long after the blood has left the brain that conceived them. Future repasts from humanity's kitchen are cooked from leftovers: glyphs, lines, or marks; chiseled stones, scrolls, and stelae. The prehistorian reads documents of bone; the historian's are more prosaic (even if, what survives of the past not being the same as perfect knowledge of it, history as a science is not simple memory but memory's criticism). The trace figures strategically in the species' passage toward humanness through permanent self-education. Diffusing, circulating, and broadcasting signs or symbols (alphabetic, textual, or audiovisual) at a distance is secondary to setting them down. If the first process allows a change of civilization, the second engenders nothing less than civilization itself, that is, the *translatio*, brightening the future and lighting the way of a past into a present.

What is the remnant when all is forgotten? The object. To entrust a performance that perishes to a base material that endures is the least uncertain means of putting it across space and time. Life makes itself over into duration, into perdurability and long life—or self-consciousness—by means of nonliving materials, things without consciousness. A human primate who left nothing tangible after him would return to the condition of the great apes. Not that the constituent materials of spirituality or idealization escape natural disintegration; archives too are subject to general entropy, to pollution or microorganisms. Papyrus is destroyed by humidity, parchment by fire, paper by acid, vinyl records by heat, magnetized tape by demagnetizing, and so on. Ornamental gardens dry up, forged steel corrodes, marble rubs and chips away, tapestries fade, stained glass loses color to the wash of rain. Bacteria, molds and fungi, viruses, and algae gnaw away at the surface of solid materials, hence the efforts of research labs, art curators, inspectors of historical monuments, and France's Direction du patrimoine to preserve them. The fact remains that inanimate matter is more reliable than organic matter, and monument less uncertain than embalmment, because mausolea last longer than mummies. Would we contain things truly memorable without those things we call monuments, our only architectural forms lacking all apparent utility?

The *monumentum*—a genre that can range from the medallion to the tribal fetish and from the museum to the hard disk—stages revivals more than survivals. Thus it is with the monuments to the dead of our small towns, which are less declarations of piety toward those lost to war than admonitions addressed to the survivors, should it come to that, to die nobly for their country. Underneath the Latin *moneo* ("I warn") lies in state the Greek root *men*, "mind" or "soul."[14] It is bound up with the paradox of mind as its own subject, having to make itself present to itself by putting a distance from itself into the object. (And here it is a shame that the Malraux of the "Museum Without Walls" in his *Voices of Silence* chose to remove so completely the domain of forms from that of mechanical techniques, when in fact the history of materiality imposes structure and rhythm on that of the imaginary.) By materializing my experience, I detach it from myself and allow it to survive me. I extract it from its experiential context and thus make it available to others, infinitely usable and appropriable (by whoever possesses the code). I pass on the intransitive. I virtually make my singularity collective, enabling a future collective to make a return to the past and to identify me now (then) as having been singular. I give power of attorney to others to live and think vicariously what I lived or thought. And I myself cannot internalize anything but what has been externalized before me, in such a manner that the link from within one person to the inwardness of another who is not yet born will be made via an outwardness, a crafted materiality, a witness to the great relay race of generations.

The animal's capacity to leave a chemical signal (such as secretions from the glands or deposits of urine), in its difference from vocal or gestural signaling, can doubtless be likened to an embodied memory, enabling as it does a message to be decoded in the sender's absence exactly like a written trace. Yet this constitutes little more than a hint or piece of bait, for the detachable human memory requires the hand-tool pairing to intervene functionally. Would the human faculty to symbolize meaning—something of which the species is justifiably proud—draw anything of consequence for its descendants if there were not superadded to it the capacity to leave the symbols as a cultural legacy? This second faculty requires concretization such as *recorded* witnessing, *written-down* discourse, gestures *preserved* in stone or lines. A surface of inscription converts time into space. It is the captured infrequency of what will never come again that, making cries into words and signal into sign, dynamically promotes the value of the occasional. The short of it is that the human race would have no intellectual and spiritual history if it had not learned first how to transform matter into artifact.

Let me venture a generalization that flies in the face of our recent superstitions: if a code can be animal, the technologies for taking it down and preserving it can only be human. The queen bee, *apis mellifera*, makes use of a highly sophisticated language at once visual, auditory, and olfactory to inform her fellow creatures about sources of food supply through a subtle combination of "danced" shapes that her followers decode. Dolphin, chimpanzee, or bee, the animal communicates, but it does not record traces, engrave, carve, or etch them. It emits signals but keeps no archives. It follows all sorts of complicated paths, but it does not build roads. It leaves biodegradable carcasses in the open air but digs and marks no graves to render the remains they contain psychodegradable in the deepest thoughts of the survivors. (To bury someone is to give memorable and perennial form to that which will soon no longer have one.) The carrier pigeon orients itself better than we do to the solar hour; it also manufactures no gnomons or sextants. Warm-blooded mammals have territories, but they set up no customs or frontier posts. Somewhere between merely journeying and making traces or, if you will, between simply making one's way and making *a* way, between path and road, there corresponds a change of lineage along living creatures' branch of descent. All indications are that the human miracle consists in *making meaning material*, the reverse side and paradoxical complement of the birth of intellect.[15] This is the real achievement, the Rubicon that separates (anthropoid) intelligence from (human) mindfulness and spirituality. *Objects*, removable and transferable, now make their appearance in the landscape. An animal is surrounded only by *things*. The anthropological criterion is, properly speaking, the artifact as mediation between the human and the material (Bernard Stiegler). Can one encompass with a single theoretical sweep the entirety of mediating artifacts and artifice that guarantee, within determinate environments, a transmission of meaning? It would have to include a grouping whose elements, simultaneously and one by one, connected man to man and man to matter. And it would be the ideal way to go about understanding their functions mediologically. Its hypotheses would allow one to pinpoint what separates and what is shared between den and dwelling, herd or pack and group, migratory course or rounds in a habitat and road, ecological niche and public space, or, if one prefers, the tool *user* we identify the superior mammal to be and the tool *maker* that is *Sapiens sapiens*. There would we very probably find, in their shadowy silence, the missing links that would enable us to move from the biological to the cultural (and within academic disciplinary space, from an ethology to an ethnology).[16]

The discovery of old human remains in the African savannah has pushed back the beginnings of hominization to four or five million years. Discussion continues among prehistorians, notably stimulated by the works of Yves Coppens, about the paths and stages of the hominid branch up to the appearance of the first cities toward 5000 B.C. This beach of time is immense by historical reckoning, minuscule on the geologic scale. On it, on dual planes technologic and symbolic, unfolded the progressive conquering of space and time, so many steps along the way of human technogenesis. By morphologically reconstructing the logical complex of these breakthroughs at each level or plateau of development, André Leroi-Gourhan showed practically that as the hominid discovered its humanness through its functional operations with basic necessities, technology invented man as much as man invented technology. If, in François Jacob's formulation, man is "preprogrammed" to learn, can one not venture an initial approximation by classifying as technical or technological every activity that does not figure directly in the program? Speaking is a natural disposition: normally constituted human beings articulate; there is no society without speech. Setting down speech is a technological activity: phonetic notation of thought is not written into the genome. There are reasons to argue that such recording is neither originary nor, once acquired, universal. There have been societies without writing; others, that lack the vocalic alphabet and use ideograms. Our linear writing style does not partake of the species' biologic lot but is rather a local invention, contingent in time, that might not have come about under different circumstances. Let us indeed be on our guard not to commit "the fundamental mistake of thinking that there is technique only when there is an instrument" (or an apparatus or machine), as Marcel Mauss advises in "Les techniques du corps" (1936). There are technical methods and masteries of dancing, walking, rocking babies, and carrying loads, one's own body being "man's first and most natural instrument."[17] Besides these, there are also cognitive tools and systems (counting, writing, etc.) involving no visible equipment, as there are effective ritualistic actions that require no tools or utensils ready to hand.

I will not detail here how Mauss's ex-pupil Leroi-Gourhan found a way to demonstrate and describe, without spiritualistic or teleological speculations, each evolutionary stage at which brain and hand worked in coordination, from the enlargement of the cranial vault and reduction of mammalian prognathism, sloping forehead, and heavy brow ridge of the frontal bone, with rounding out of the skull's posterior part, all the way to the computer. Instead, I shall attempt to grasp the spirit and gist of it.

The author of the prehistoric sites of Pincevent and Arcy-sur-Cure theorized as a linked continuum biological evolution, technological progress, and social organization, without failing to distinguish between the three levels but also without separating the sector of language from the sector of tools. The use of both is connected neurologically and emerges at the same cultural stages. In 35,000 B.C.—at the end of the third (Riss-Würm) interglacial period, when Mousterian (Middle Paleolithic)-type cultural remains are found in strata of the Upper Pleistocene geological stage—there appear coloring agents, the first rhythmically graphic marks, burial at gravesites, and stone hatchets. Around 6000 B.C., there is evidence of agricultural settlement, metallurgy, writing, and villages. In other words, there was simultaneity of technologies and language. Showing the codeterminations of the face-hand complex, this skillful comparative chronologist could announce in 1960 the latest inventions of the century's end (hypertext, virtual reality, and sedentary cyberglobetrotting) because he knew how to relate on the same plane the polished pebble and the small screen, Neolithic gravesites and the culture industries.[18]

How did Leroi-Gourhan bring this off? He singled out, within the long time span of evolutionary tendencies, certain technological lines of development centering around externalizing the inside, according to a scale of diminishing energy expenditures relative to tasks accomplished. This meant, in succession, the exteriorization of human skeletal functions into edged silex stone scrapers, choppers, and hand axes; of human muscles into animal traction, water wheels, and windmills; of language into writing; of counting into calculating machines (pebble systems, abacus, etc.); and of imaginative faculties into film and television. Technology is anchored in biology, and tools are the fruit not of intelligence but of life. It is when brain size reached its largest volume (fifteen hundred cubic centimeters) that the utensil saw a startling advancement. The average overequipped human in a prosperous country in the year 2000 will have the same number of neurons as the Neanderthal thirty thousand years ago, but the process of evolution has leapt from its somatic fortress to gallop freely in externalities. The creeping pace of passage from fish to australopithecine, from Primary to Quaternary, did not stop there. It kept on accelerating, from flake tools to nuclear power stations, in the short interval of time separating *Zinjanthropus* from modern symbiotic man.

Thus is there an inexorable commonality between the evolution of technologic equipment and that composite cavalcade of invertebrates, warm-blooded mammals, and primates with already completely hominid dentition (for who needs long canines when flint can do most of the preliminary work?). It does render humanistic and creationist recriminations a bit futile. For both hominids and tools, there is an acceleration of the stream's current and an identity of direction from simple to complex. The body of *Homo faber* "exuded" its tools almost in the same fashion as its own claws, binding itself to matter and assimilating its environment's energy sources to the point of putting together a kind of artificial envelope, a more and more complex, thickening layer of intermediary organs by means of which, and across which, he protects, nourishes, and transports himself (consuming his wood with the adze, his meat with the knife, etc.). We have never had an immediate relation to nature but rather one that was straight away mediated by devices and symbols.

Why are we so overequipped technoculturally? Because we are *under*equipped physioanatomically, inadequately specialized. It is the hand's weakness that gives rise to and calls for the tool. Had we possessed the internal clock of the carrier pigeon, we would not have needed to invent the water clock nor the astronomical compass. Suited to everything yet immediately good for nothing: with this distinctive quality the biped in its newly upright position, who represented such a brush with nature's error, profited from erring itself to become polyvalent, omnivorous, functionally opportunistic, prone to frequent travel and roaming widely, and adaptable to all climates and habitats (Homo sapiens is the only animal species distributed on all five continents). "Thou shalt perish from thy virtues and triumph by thy vices," predicted Nietzsche. Did this throw off balance the phylogenetic line, or was it instead its crowning achievement?

One might say it was both or that the achievement followed from the imbalance. It takes an ox forty-seven days to double its birth weight, a horse sixty, a human one hundred eighty. Under its environment's selective pressures, Homo sapiens's delayed biological maturation causes a considerable advance in compensatory acculturation. Our hereditary behaviors' very weaknesses transfer the species' odds of survival to acts of transmitting culture, more particularly to educating the young (who are dependent on the adults for a longer time than their anthropoid cousins). Thus to the famous question "What does man lack to prevent his remaining an animal?" the reply can almost be given, "A substantial genetic endowment," a lack made over by the theft of fire into a comparative advantage.

Such would be the underlying kernel of rationality in the myth of Prometheus from Plato's *Protagoras*. His impious exploit, it must not be forgotten, stemmed not from pride but from the mistake made by his brother Epimetheus, the scatterbrain who, having emptied his gift sack of qualities to bestow on the animals and found none left to bequeath to men, left the latter stragglers deprived of essences. Strength went to lions, speed to antelopes, hooves to quadrupeds, fur to bears. Nothing was left over for the unfledged creature on two feet. It was indeed imperative that fire be given to these disabled runts of morphology's litter so that they might at least survive. In his inspired and precise commentary on this foundational myth (and without Prometheus there could have been no Faust), Bernard Stiegler's *Technics and Time* has brought to light the relation obtaining between "mortals' originary 'technicity' " and their "original lack."[19] This technological prosthesis, despite the origin of the word in the Greek for "to add to," was not a simple added portion or anodyne accessory: it set the whole human relay race on its way. One says of the technological world that it has become our second nature, yet since there never was an unmediated first nature, humans never had any choice in the matter. Human being in the world is secondhand to start with.

The relative stagnation of our organic, morphological equipment since the emergence of Neanderthal hominids—the remains of whose cranial vaults and musculoskeletal frames we conserve and measure—has had as its counterpart an explosively prolific extension of numerous artifacts of enablement and facilitation in the world external to the immediate human body. And though it may be true that the faculty of individual memory has indeed diminished with our graphic and representational mnemonic devices, as Plato forecast in the *Phaedrus* by tallying the effects and ill effects of the god Toth's discovery, this localized loss is more than compensated for by the formidable accumulation of extracerebral memory represented by humankind's collective technical systems. Now the miraculous and dangerous consequence of these performances is that externalized memory, considered in its aspect of work and potential, has no assignable limits. Their lack throws open an endless working-out of forces wherein the end-of-history thesis is nonsense, technology being that which cannot not reopen and revive history. A countless number of changes spring from it, on which no foreseeable ceiling can be set (if not certain parameters of physics such as the speed of light). More abrasive force will always be marshaled by a windmill than by my fingernails, more information stored up in my library than in my neurons, more mathematical functions on a silicon chip than in Einstein's brain.

This capacity for expansion distinguishes occasional instrumentation (such as a chimp's stacking boxes to climb toward a banana) from the achievements of human arts and crafts. An artificial organ surpasses all improvised functionality by carrying within it an entire tradition, that is, the entire series of deeds that led to producing it and those other enactments required by each new instance of putting resources to use. (This operational chain of causes and effects was already implied in the presence of that element of self-conscious knowing, *sapiens*, in the older *Homo faber*, just as mental calculation was already implied in the most minimal technological gesture.) Unlike the instrument, which can be used up in its immediate application, the tool is manufactured before and conserved after acts of its utilization. Even the most rudimentary kind of tool functions as a memory minder. A biface (hand axe) recognizably chipped into an almond shape is truly a deposit and vector of culture, the bearer of a learned competency (technique of percussion) that was extended and reproduced from one generation of rock choppers to the next. A properly mediological inquiry, hypothetically arriving at a methodological consistency one hundred years down the road from our bricolage, could begin its itinerary not with the first stone surfaces covered with abstract signs but with the silex scraper of the lower Paleolithic one hundred thousand years earlier, the first attested creation of culture. It would allow us to scrutinize our own ideological landscape with the cold observation of a gravesite excavation, scrupulously reconstituting such and such a vanished mentality through its material culture and the work of the concrete remains (hewn and polished pebbles, bones, bronzes, etc.), deducing its internal structures from the external manipulations, the plausible deployments, of its vestiges. This would turn up so many mutations, hybridizations, and drifts, and without a moralizing verdict.

A vast distance separates this mastery of detachment from our exploratory gropings. But let the record show all the same that the most seminal of our extraliterary sources of influence (if we exclude Diderot, Hugo, Balzac, and the prophetic Paul Valéry) is not McLuhan, nor even Walter Benjamin (a more entitled creditor than the Canadian), but rather the genial and scandalously neglected scientific author of *L'homme et la matière*. Without having thematized transmission as a philosophicocultural category as such, this solitary scholar dared patiently and meticulously to relate achievements at the level of symbol use to those at the technical level. And so, should some exile have made available to him only a single printed work from the "Sciences of Man and Society" section of the library to take along to a desert island or into a prison cell, he would do well to pack *Gesture and Speech* in his pouch. That book is, to my knowledge, the most replete account of what Pascal called "the succession of men," an account in which the ceaseless shuttling back and forth between corporeal and mental, between vectors and values, and memories and liberations authorizes its reader to encompass reconstructively, on a level with an age-old dynamics, each combined turning point in the evolution of cortex, silex, and signs.

6

Disciplinary Imperialisms

Human beings are thus the one animal that produces a culture technologically. The prehistorian's synthesizing perception restores coherence to the long history of human evolution by showing the paradoxical unity of technological invention and social invention. The signal achievement of a Leroi-Gourhan is to have articulated the two sides of the adventure through the millennia. In this respect his work's synoptic account of humanness transcending biology with technology offers considerable incitement to the research I call on here. There is little choice, over the short term and at this juncture, but to clear a path forward through two totalizing (sometimes totalitarian) disciplinary responses to the problem of explaining cultural change and continuity. These two empirelike fields can, without unduly emphasizing the dichotomy, be called the "all-socio" and the "all-bio" poles of explanation.

Because cultural transmission operates as a common factor in both these areas, the mediological field strongly resembles a crossroads. It borders, first and obviously, on two explanatory systems that lie like disciplinary massifs, one overlooking it from above (namely, sociology) and the other reaching its conclusions from below (biology). These two poles of rational inquiry remain opposed, at the far ends of a human fact itself indivisible, where the threads of social relations and neurological connections, cultural codes and a genetic code, weave together in a manner that is still obscure. It would be a highly artificial clarification to lay them out in perfect symmetry with one another simply to dispense with each in short order. I feel my approach to be conspicuously closer to, and more implicated by, the diverse sociologies of culture, art, science, or education than the many variants of sociobiology in the mode of Edward O. Wilson. With the search for a third way already owing a debt to numerous social sciences (beginning with the history of mentalities, technology, and cultural practices), it would, besides, be ungracious for this line of research to prepare indictments without the theoretical means to back them up. At the least it is still obliged to indicate both where it depends on previous research and why it stands out.

It is not a matter of arguing over the recognized gains of scientific knowledge (whose validity is uncontested if of uneven value), in the manner of those strategies of distancing that tend, in Bourdieu's terms, to add the technical profits that derive from free borrowings to the symbolic profits of humanistic refusal. Rather, one must find the proper articulation, the imbrications or interlockings, between different levels of reality. Mediology's approach has its reasons that Reason of the sociological or biological persuasion neither wishes, nor can, nor should know, inasmuch as its validity begins or terminates their critical space of pertinence. Its space comes into its own by a decentering: in its purview, what appears central and consistent will be held by a sociologist, for example, to be marginal and not relevant, according to his critical principles for isolating what matters. An example is technological equipment; another, the particular constraints of a given environment of cultural transmission or mediasphere, conditioned historically.

THE RISKS OF "ALL-SOCIO"

"The property of living being is that it makes its own habitat, composes it."[1] Let us observe first that man does not compose his habitat in an arbitrary way but as a function of biological imperatives typical to him, a contingent but constraining given. "Had man possessed dentition suited to grinding plant material and a ruminant's gut, the bases of sociology would have turned out radically different."[2] Teeth for both tearing and grinding and a simple stomach orient survival toward the consumption of animal flesh, whose living providers are scattered naturally over the landscape, imposing a certain relation to space and thus a certain mode of organizing into groups. This ruled out the kinds of mass seasonal migrations to summer pastures particular to herbivores, entailing the frequentation of a defined territory, with its fixed settings for hunting game that vary with seasonal cycles. Such would be an example of native constraints—that is, originating from the food-territory-density relation—that a sociological approach cannot fail to abstract (being obligated otherwise to take account of an infinite regression of causal factors). The historian, however, imagines what kind of impact on relations of domination between the sexes this prehistoric specialization of tasks could have had. Might it not have tended to associate men with the tasks of hunting and women with picking and gathering, deriving these differentiations from a quest for food whose exigencies were determined physiologically (and much more markedly than in the world of the higher animals)?

Generally speaking, then, it is the conditions in which each organism finds it necessary to capture living matter that set up a confrontation with its physical environment, obliging it, for its own survival, to negotiate technologically with that environment. Culture comes on the scene as the product of constant scumbling between an inside and an outside, insofar as Homo sapiens adapts to his surroundings by the medium of a tooled membrane, a set of external organs, and a metabolizing, reinforced infrastructure or underwiring. Across this living frame, he regulates his exchanges with the deposits of energy that surround him. Life has been described as a continuous conquest of mobility, the forfeit of stability that must be made if one is to have growing autonomy vis-à-vis the immediate environment. So too is the featherless biped locomotive: he surveys a territory, spies food sources, observes the sky night and day, opens up roads, builds bridges. For the sociologist, as for the historian, these things go all too often without saying. For a mediologist, it is better to say them. And the concrete means of locomotion, along with the courses, channels, and tracks of communication, become a cynosure of focus, a problematic tangle to untangle.

Not counting the fact that sociologists pay heed not to cavemen but to complex societies, every epistemological framework shapes the world's plenum to its windows of perception and reflection. Sociology would never have become a distinct discipline if social organizations could be easily folded into specific needs and functions, and it is the concrete variations of invariable biologic functions (such as domination, sexuality, territory, acquisition, and aggressiveness) that are of such interest to Leroi-Gourhan, the descendant of Durkheim and Max Weber. Against the rich spectrum of extant social forms, our common basis of flesh and bone has no explanatory basis because it is always and everywhere self-identical. This is self-evident. But it is sometimes necessary to revisit our zoological contingency back upstream in time, if one is intent on getting past the high-tech utopia of an artificially produced environment-medium shorn of any of the classic animal and material constraints. Superstitions of the Tool overvalue the novel effects of technological innovation, by incessantly reviving emancipatory expectations incessantly disappointed. This is therefore an opportune moment, by recalling foundational archaisms, to be able to thwart some of the poor man's millenarianism that takes hold among the rich as they behold each new technologic leap. (Celebrations of a planetary honeymoon of democracy and information on the World Wide Web are its latest version.) To this end, it can never hurt to be reminded, by one observer of the long durations, that "no fundamental difference separates the bird's tufted crest from the helmet's ornamental plume, the cock's spur from the nobleman's saber, or the pigeon's bowing and scraping from the gallantries of a country dance" and that "our electronic culture, hardly fifty years on this earth, is still based materially in a physiological apparatus that goes back forty thousand years."[3] At least a few of tomorrow morning's disillusions might be spared by keeping in mind that today's symbiotic cyberman still works from the same rhinencephalon, or olfactory system of the brain, as did the stalker of wool-ly mammoths in the Paleolithic, that predatory mammal with eyes glued to the horizon of his secured perimeter and endowed with a specieswide aggression that served him so well in defending it. The wider pyramidal view of evolutionary variation inclines one to temper enthusiasm whipped up by the latest bright and liberatory prospects of fevered celebrants of the neo-cortex (be it externalized or not into software). No matter how much our newest tools will have projected onto the horizon a shimmering mirage of planetary society—a transparent, pedagogic paradise wholly given over to peaceful exchanges of information—that obscene, rhinencephalonic under-layer will persist in claiming its portion of blood and mud. Every last moth-er's child, slipped from her belly's soft shackles, will forever after have to face down the crouching carnivore within, but, luckily for it, not without a help-ing hand from the tools of civilization.

Underestimating the biological conditioning of the only animal that has a history may cause one to overlook its modes of connecting and adjusting itself to its physical environment. Technology is what allows a living being to gain purchase and maintain a hold on its surroundings. An observation by Lucien Febvre's in 1935 bears repeating, namely, that technology is one of those numerous words with which history is not made and history of tech-nology one of those numerous disciplines still entirely to be created. Attention has been paid since then to the admonishment. Contemporaries and successors of the Annales school's founder have examined such things as the waterwheel and turning millstone (Marc Bloch); animal traction and the yoke, harness, and their towing attachments (Lefebvre des Nouettes); the rudder and tiller and instruments of nautical navigation (Braudel); and time measurement and the mechanical clock (Landes). And the history of technology, for all its remove from the nobler history of mentalities (and from biographies and the popular history of sites of memory) has managed to find its niche somewhere in the institution's side aisles.

One idea we have of sociology—and it may by now be passé, superseded by the Centre de sociologie de l'innovation at the Ecole des Mines—can give the impression that, as far as critical sociology is concerned, the railroad, the automobile, or the microwave oven are still struggling for legitimacy as objects of study among Durkheim's descendants. When it comes to the telegraph, photography, forms of transportation, radio waves, or virtual reality, the sociological establishment throughout this century appears to have readily off-loaded such alien subjects onto the sciences of communication, a bazaar open to all comers. True, nobody can be at the bakery and the mill at the same time, and not analyzing a phenomenon is not to deny its existence. Things nonetheless continue to take place as though we remain unconsciously prone and driven to decouple study of the *socius* from its artificial ecosystem (especially the industrial processes of extracting, storing, and distributing energy), the study of institutions having traditionally had the jump on that of technical systems. As if coal supplies and utilization lived a life on one side, and the proletarian worker on the other. As if movable lead type's antiquation concerned only printed materials and not the organizational modes of salaried workers (the newspaper as collective organizer). And as if France's division into departmental administrative units had nothing at all to do with the common use of saddled horses, or the creation of distinct regions today with the kinds of travel encouraged by highways. Historians know full well one cannot speak of the nineteenth century's popular culture without referring to its rail system, of mass flows of information without mentioning electricity, of the "Image Civilization" without discussing the distinct properties of electromagnetic tape recording and the cathode ray tube. The sociogenesis of actions persists in overshadowing the technogenesis of the social, as if modern sociology remained more beholden to the philosophical grand tradition than it cares to admit to itself.

It is true that technological revolutions do not deduce in linear fashion from a first principle. Largely unpredictable and always unforeseen, imperceptible in their initial surge and then confusing in their fallout effects, they oblige a thinker to exile himself outside thought to embrace contingency. The telephone; the vinyl, floppy, or hard disk; photosensitive paper; the silicon chip: these will all appear to that person's eyes to be poor objects unworthy of considered meditation. Besides, he or she will have hardly had time to form a theory of the object in question, to have located for it a small place in the system, before a second object, of the next generation, will have come along after ten years to contradict the laborious speculative effort, forcing a return to the drawing board. Pursuing such a course proves not only arduous but also humiliating for the great author worthy of the title. Subsequently, when the given technological innovation rapidly separates from its site of invention, it seems to lose all sociological interest by soon affecting all the other sites. And this happens even if the diffusion of the new device or system is socially determined. (For example, the automobile tended rather to go *down* the scale of social class, while television has climbed *up* it.) We do owe sociology for understanding, against all technological determinism, that every social group assimilates technological innovation in its own manner, according to its own rhythm (which may be a delayed one) and its own codes (which may also lag), and that it is a far cry from any potential application of an apparatus to the utilization that actually comes about. Technology's promise is one thing; how it is appropriated, another. A worker exacts from the telephone different services from those exacted by a society hostess; the popular classes do not use cameras for snapshots in the same way that aesthetes do. Each person negotiates on a small scale with the challenge of a technologized world. The first impulse of the sociologist confronting these phenomena will not, however, be to ask what distinguishes them from their older versions or what they supersede within the evolutionary chain of inventions and functional dynamics out of which they arose. Rather, the sociologist ends up looking for the social causality they mask or the class stereotypes they reproduce. An unexpected technological development will not be seen as a significant historical departure but as a mirror of collective forces, a signal confirming meanings elsewhere, a pretext to let the social speak. Wanting too much to demystify the fetishism of tools and equipment, we lose sight of their very reality.

We are in the debt of sociology's pioneers for their having collectivized, sometimes to excess, the individual subject; it falls to the students of technology to *individualize the collective object.* The technologic object's strange "mode of existence" (Simondon) culminates in those expanding macrosystems (highway, railway, aeronautic, electrical systems, etc.) empowered with such a capacity for adaptation and self-regulation that, once they have an assured place in the ecosystem, they resemble quasi-creatures. As in the case of the spongelike growth of the Internet, they seek to increase themselves at the expense of the surrounding environment by annexing the competing subsystems. These automations seem to obey their own finality, persevering in being.[4] And as prostheses of human functions, they control our social, imaginary, and concrete existence. This is something poets and novelists knew before philosophers. Mac Orlan concludes, for example, that the internal combustion engine changes the sentimental givens of life.

To Durkheim's foundational question, "On what is social cohesion *based?*" a completely sociological answer can no longer suffice, insofar as the century that now separates us from that disciplinary constitution has brought to the fore the shaping force of our technological structurings. The social scientist's social facts today would no longer be comparable to things of nature but rather to successive montages of invented devices. A megasystem of technical systems (or a complex scaffolding of artifacts) resembles the realm of natural objects in that such a system, like Durkheim's transcendent social order, cannot be modified by a simple decree of the will (Durkheim, *Rules*). Machineries' perpetually rising power unveils retrospectively the underlying material mechanism of preceding states of society, however crude and primitive but no less imperious it may appear to later generations. When we take full account of such a mechanism, we must adjust accordingly our calibrations of the zone constraining human actors. What imposes itself on individuals with an irresistible force is not ultimately collective behaviors, institutions, beliefs, and representations, for the reason that the coercive, imperative power by whose virtue they impose themselves on the individual (Durkheim) does not properly belong to them. The obliging force resides in the mechanical systems and networks (the mediasphere) that sustain social phenomena's existence but whose dynamic eludes the powers and agents endeavoring to relay it among individual persons. Despite the costs of doing so, we have had to take cognizance of the technologic fact's *normative power*, one that is usurped, perhaps, but that remains above the power of the social fact that mediates it. Somewhere in its precincts is where the profound order that Michelet contrasted with the known, limited, and narrowly prudent order where authority lodges must be sought. To this displacement of actual lines of force corresponds logically a displacement of lines of research, including research in sociology (notably of art, sciences, and industry).

The dimension sociology has missed calls up more than a merely supplemental tool kit, the equivalent in terrestrial terms to theology's bodily supplement of the fully formed soul. The direct object of actions is inherent in the subject's very constitution, and the "what" elaborates the "who" (Bernard Stiegler).[5] There is not, for example, *first* the feeling of personal identity, stable and primordial, and *then* the changing play of its various objectivizations. The mirror or polished stone, the signature by hand, silent reading of text to oneself, the portrait (a portable image of the self), the identity card photo (a reproducible duplicate): all these inventive matrices, however dated, left their stamp and made their lasting impression on human interiority. Our subjective presence to ourselves is engendered by our objective representations, and the ego's image is knitted into being from objective traces, as are our mental images from our objective picturings. The self is manufactured night and day by its objective products as much as by its dreams (which by means of phantasms enchant our phantoms unmoving and animated).

If the social configurations of subjectivity are themselves configured by the technological infrastructures of the social, so many of our personal dispositions translate devices and systems whose marks have been left on mentalities (for example, habits that have been justly called "mechanical"). Our style of walking, observed Marcel Mauss, was never the same after the cinematograph: young women in Paris learned to sway their hips like their Hollywood models.[6] The belfry clock or the church bell, the calendar, and the wristwatch, as well as the map or the kilometer marker on the side of the road, all heavily influence our intuitive sense of duration and spatial extension. Likewise do we delegate our mental faculties to contrivances that aid human memory, such that losing one's daily planner causes serious trouble, misplacing one's glasses means losing one's vision, and removing one's shoes takes away meaningful locomotion. The symbol-enabled mastery of time itself (through forecasting, planning, and management) supposes practices of material inscription.[7] Have we not seen so far, however, eminent sociologists of industrial and postindustrial societies reserve a more than succinct place for technologies? It is true that a new generation of researches is taking care to refer ideas back to tools.[8] All this is a welcome antidote to a sociologism that, as soon as one takes up its practice, threatens (as did its founding fathers) to reduce medium to means and innovation to mere gadgetry. The same duality, rational-activity-in-its-finality versus rational-activity-in-its-value, leads Max Weber from the outset, for example, to define the "technics" of an activity as the sum of means necessary to its exercise, in opposition to the activity's meaning or end or purpose, which in the final analysis determines (concretely speaking) its orientation.[9] The real drama, however, judging from the course the world takes, is that a technological mediation has a direction or orientation already incorporated into its substance, the means carrying the end along with it. How not to reach the conclusion that today finalities do not precede or survive technological outfittings with the lofty superiority our moralizing humanism rather off-handedly assigned to them? The Internet is a market-driven ideology, normative and prescriptive. And television is as well, in the same capacity as the telephone and movable type printing long ago.

A sterling illustration of sociological arrogance, manifested in its refusal to delve deeper into and even respect at all the technological object's rebellious and tenacious strangeness, can be found in the currently most fashionable discourse about the low status of television, popularized by Pierre Bourdieu's best-selling book on it.[10] This sociologist considers the subject to be released from all need for further probing once he has made it clear that telejournalists who are most in the spotlight exhibit a strong tendency toward conformity, that the major networks in France belong to dominant groups, that one hardly has time to develop one's ideas when they appear in this medium, that we always see the same talking heads (who are all ostensibly in cahoots with one another), that face-to-face confrontations are a kind of trompe l'oeil, and that television is abusively stifling written forms of communication and print media. We must be grateful to a specialized sociological idiom for transforming such commonly recognized self-evidences—which specialists in the matter have been going on about now for three decades—into critical discoveries. More seriously, constraints that weigh heavily on the TV medium are imputed to the social relations of a professional milieu, taken as a reflection of the relations of force that prevail in a global society. In this vein, the self-fulfilling construct of a "journalistic field," by virtue of its minimally operative generality, dissolves practical and very real distinctions that otherwise need to be made among the circulating daily newspaper, the illustrated periodical, and around-the-clock audiovisual coverage, just as it turns to abstraction the operative determinations of a medium's material base (paper, electronic screen, or digital interface), the technical information-delivery system (postal service, air waves, or satellites), as well as the semiotic codes proper to the various channels for broadcasting information and representations (written signs, living speech, or animated imagery). Yet all these are decisive details that concretely determine the object.

In such manner, the intrinsic properties *of* television are evacuated by the discourse *on* it. Lost from view is the multidetermined singularity of a very specific machine, along with the production constraints that result from it and are incorporated into every possible application of it. In the end, however, narrow parameters of economic viability mark out this heavy industry. Still, critical sociology, which prides itself on being sincerely demystifying (and can indeed be so in political terms, with fortunate ideological effects further down the stream of causal consequence), idolizes into a postulate far back upstream, without any prior critical clarification, the mystifying preconception of technology as pure instrumentality characteristic of classical idealism (including all its successor philosophies of a materialist stamp). This is doubtless why the least technologically informed consideration of what distin-guishes, for example, the electronic image and its rhythms of flow from other kinds of images and even of the possible meanings of technology itself can all be passed over in silence, in an intellectual calculation of profit and loss, by the sociologist Bourdieu, who claims to present in clear and synthesized form the acquired knowledge of research carried out on the subject of television.

THE RISKS OF "ALL-BIO"

Naturalism's reductionist understanding of culture is at the opposite pole from sociological reductionism. How does it answer an extremist sociology, without any biological or geographical basis, that propounds a wholly social construction of reality? With an excessive biologism that leaves history and society behind, the interpretation one ends up with in those highly regard-ed research programs that use the natural selection model to approach cul-tural phenomena.[11] Whatever the heuristic richness of such a model, it can easily veer off, via unilateralism, to phantasmagoric extrapolations (which professional biologists are in fact the first to criticize). Here the overly holis-tic fundamentalism consists in denying the objective existence of objects the researcher must exclude from the field of research, namely, those nonor-ganic entities constituted by organized matter (tools and material bases) and materialized organizations (norms and institutions).

In every age, psychology has seemed fated to seek its salvation by importing formal models outside itself. As François Dagognet has noted, "Psychology has inevitably, successively, applied to subjectivity certain technologies and scientific representations refined by their own success elsewhere."[12] With Descartes, psychology was mechanistic; with Locke and Condillac, Newtonian; with Taine, trivially chemical; now it is informa-tional. The explanatory system that goes under the prestigious name of cognitive psychology and is sometimes borrowed from molecular biology presently sets its sights on deriving benefits from the transfer of two para-digms, cybernetic and genetic, with the latter providing a distinct advan-tage as it is more recent and cost-effective in its organicist efficiency.[13]

Within the neurosciences, the axis of brain-psyche has already proven its uncontestable fecundity. To extrapolate these kinds of applications by con-structing a brain-society axis, short-circuiting the intermediate stages, per-haps comes under the heading of a rash intellectual wager. The temptation is great, when a new era does not yet exactly recognize what kind of world it is entering into, to apply, at an as-yet inadequately known and complex level, models that have already been tested in a wider or less precisely specialized application (not to forget the old, illuminating, and simple model of Darwinian selection). By such co-optation, it will seem enough to assimilate, first, cultural phenomena to cerebral mechanisms and, second, these latter to the reproductive mechanisms of life. Might not one call biologism—these growing pains of sciences of culture—such a transposition of one given epistemological framework into another that has admitted propinquity with the first but is not identical with it?

This said, how can one not end up subscribing to the initial idea that holds there is no ineffable metaphysical entity to be fit under the term *culture*? Something should become operative in our field similar to what biology brought about just yesterday: replacing the opaque entity called "vital force" by the discrete, identifiable units of living being. There are several good intentions here that do in fact look like the preconditions of rational advance in the study of man: demystifying the rhetoric of mere instrumentality; closing the gap between natural and human sciences; removing psychology from the myths of interiority and enthrallments to ego, so that research and approaches might become more objectively materialist; reconceptualizing the social by means of population models based on averages; moving, as a positivistic researcher, from *interpretation* to *explanation*, from a mystery to a problem, from hermeneutic incantations to experimental models of natural causation, without being intimidated by that reactionary blackmail label of opprobrium, "Reductionism!" (a classic quibble of lazy minds).

Everyone can appreciate and welcome the progress that the cognitive sciences have brought to improving our knowledge of brain functioning and, more widely, the processing of information in all its forms. One cannot count it among the least of their merits that they have broken through the fences between disciplines that stifle research and expanded competencies while aiming toward a long-awaited hybridization between so-called hard and soft sciences. It is not hard to make out the potential fertility of an approach that reintegrates culture within evolutionary change (without dashing the former against the harshest determinisms of the latter, certainly). Still, "cognisciences" will not make good on their promises, it seems, by merely reviving a reifying associationist psychology as old as Condillac's *idéologie* and a substantialist or immemorial materialism à la Holbach and Helvetius. Even as a strain of this is making its way back to Europe from across the Atlantic, beefed up with probabilistic models and statistical constructions, there is warrant in not seeing in it an earth-shaking novelty. In his *Technics and Time*, Bernard Stiegler has already noted how the mechanistic modeling of human cognition shrugs off the realities of time and technology (that is, mediology's two fundamental parameters). Besides this, it is a paradox of the cognitive sciences that they are refusing to consider any in-depth rumination on technological facts at the same moment that they are promoting technology into an explanatory model of the mind's functional processes. When it is biologized, cogniscientific transmission is indifferent to vehiculation as a material fact; it takes place without paths or real time over which to spread, without either the *volumen* or the *codex*, caravans or libraries, schools of thought or churches, clubs or political parties. Its study by certain currents of cognitive psychology accredits itself with the necessary abstractness of any analytical operation, such that it never lowers itself to concrete history and remains "neurochemically pure" (on the assumption that only nature can explain nature).

Sacrificing the cultural legacy's technological basis (in materially conserved and transmitted traces) to the chemical basis of heredity and proceeding by analogy, the biologist of culture sets off on a quest for discrete units analogous to those of genetic information (the pairs of nucleotides contained in DNA). In this way he will be able to apply to cultural evolution the models of genetic evolution, to speak of drift, matrix of transmission, and variation. Or he puts to work the random mechanism of Mendel's laws, importing statistical fluctuations into the context of ideas. These characters, or cultural traits, set up as units of cultural transmission, will then be christened variously (as Dawkinsian "memes," or "cultgens," or "culturons"). Then, by a curious but classic animistic reversal that consists of taking things of logic for the logic of things, the argument passes imperceptibly from an in modo style of reasoning to an in re realization. And after having accepted the idea that ideas behave in a given setting *like* living organisms, the "like" is dispensed with, after which cerebral representations are from now on presented to us *as* living organisms, species of viruses or anaerobic bacteria lodged in the cranium's enclave and behaving like genes responsible for reproduction: genetic structures "selfishly" reproducing by themselves by the use of individual human carriers. Is not biological evolution definable as "the differentiated survival of entities that copy each other" (Dawkins)? Their cultural stand-ins, dubbed "replicatives," become objects able to produce copies of themselves, in whose core it proves necessary to identify "mutations" (to explain innovation). One can foresee the kinds of preemptive stylistic precautions the analogy in re necessitates, in its search for a convincing ideational genetics. For only superior (diploid or paired-chromosomal) organisms reproduce by chromosomal duplication.

But are ideas sexed bacteria? Do they have parents; if so, how many? If not, how in fact are cultgens cooked up by creative cultural brews? And how does one determine the representation most apt to survive without taking into account the political, social, and technological environment? Metaphor has slipped already into myth, following the slope of an imperious naturalism. It grants license to dream of scientific solutions to the ideological problem. How most infectious diseases are transmitted is more or less known. So why should one not claim to have discovered, in the wake of genetic epidemiology, how (bad) ideas are transmitted? Couldn't we envisage, one day, prophylaxis, vaccines, perhaps quarantines? At the far end of the epidemic model one can make out, not without some trepidation, a field of social-hygienic regulation once proper surveillance of predispositions has been carried out. Does a person catch Catholicism or Lacanism like a cold or viral hepatitis?

The answer is that one does not *choose* to catch a cold but one *does* elect to become a Lacanian or Marxist; and if one converts to Catholicism or homeopathy, one wanted to. Natural selection favors gene types whose perpetuation has favorable effects on the species' conservation. It appears however that for an individual human being, adopting the Christian faith in Rome in the year 142 or the Communist faith in Paris in 1942 was ill suited to improving one's heath or prolonging one's life. Yet this did take place. It is not clear that a Darwinian model suffices to account for these kinds of group identifications.

The biomedical model might still lead us, however, to place new value on the breeding ground in which ideas propagate. But for such a study, must not the biological approach hand over its research task to anthropology? No more than human beings are equal before all diseases, even if each member of the species can contract them all (Jacques Ruffié), are *societies* equal before all ideas, even though every individual can take all of them into his or her personal possession for cultivation apart. Here too there are some climates more or less propitious, and collective temperaments more or less transmissive. Just as, on the scale of actual contagions for a given infectious agent, there exists a favorable biological environment for reproduction—a function of the individual's genetic profile and acquired immunities over the course of his life—so too are various hosting environments exposed more or less to a given ideological epidemic. The degree of exposure and susceptibility is a function of a determinable anthropological profile in which family structure in particular plays a decisive role, involving such norms as the elevated or reduced status of women, rules of inheritance that are egalitarian or not, and the rate of tolerated exogamy.

It is this heavily freighted factor, if we are to take the word of certain researchers in demography, that sets the compatibility of such and such an ideology with such and such a society. "At the planetary level, the coexistence of antagonistic values is possible," writes Emmanuel Todd. "For a given territory, certain basic cultural elements are incompatible."[14] A society in which brothers are held to be equals will be receptive to universalism; one in which they are ranked differently and where the principle of male primogeniture prevails will incline toward particularism. How familial norms are transmitted will in this case govern cultural transmission. This correlation is hard to deny and quite striking. But such a factor of selection does not hold for just *any* hereditary immunity programmed by a given system of values handed down through education and culture. Southern Europe and the Arab world, for example, both show symmetrical family practices with egalitarian rules of inheritance. Yet the first region historically hatched Marxist universalist ideologies, while the second rejected the graft. Meanwhile France and Germany, quite uniformly and until just yesterday, welcomed universalism despite their adherence to an asymmetrical family structure in which the "stem family" patrilineal system held sway. These sorts of correspondences can rationalize synthesizing trains of thought leading in interesting and unpredictable directions. But they have their limits. (Recognizing such limits does not deny them their value.) Plainly, a monocausal explanation is no explanation at all.

This observation also holds true for the reductively biologizing epidemiology approach to mentalities. Rendering an abstract representation in physicalist or physiological terms does not make it ipso facto more concrete. What is differentiated is concrete; it is the indeterminate that is abstract. In the genetic night of communicational epidemics to explain ideas' transmission, all cultural cows become gray: scientific knowledge, practical know-how, and the knowledges of being. Should it not be imperative to distinguish among the fields of ideology, culture, and science rather than treating as homogeneous entities bodies of knowledge, opinions, feelings, information, convictions, rumors, norms, passions, and values? However mixed they may be in the reality of communicational practice—a bit after the fashion of *visual* and *audio* in *audiovisual*—does not each of these registers have its singular mode of transmission? One cannot scramble together (and the list is not intended to be exhaustive): apprenticeship (school), the immersion of upbringing (family), contagion (rumor), broadcasting (print, radio, and television), one-way suggestion (film and theater), influence (of a moral authority), training (barracks), information (news), persuasion (friends), seduction (amorous or physical), hypnosis (mesmerism and somnambulism), pressure (of the immediate peer group), conditioning (of the larger environment), mothering (mother-infant symbiosis), and so on. Socially transmitted attitudes, beliefs, or desires can likewise borrow numerous sensory channels singly or in combination, such as sound waves (music, song), visual images (printed characters, painting, film), touch (braille), etc.; make use of more than one mediating structure such as institutions (school, army, church, etc.) or technological devices (printing, electronics, computers); and be contextualized in interpersonal or live interactions (the one-on-one of conversation), in direct but group-format situations (the one-to-several impersonality of the book, the lecture, or the publicly delivered address), in indirect and anonymous consumption (the all-to-all of atmospheric effects), and in personalized mass communications (the one-to-all of radio and television). In all this, *it is the particularity of conveyance that directs meaning*, the detail that is significant and appropriate to explore.

Stellar movement, to give an example from science or earlier astrological pseudoscience, is not divulged by contagion. Neither is the interindividual relation of instructor to student, which is backed up by a mediative institution, here a scholarly one, with its own constraints and history of a political nature. Thus one cannot speak of an epidemic with scientific knowledge as one can in the case of socially conveyed rumor or social emotion. Knowledge is incorporated into disciplines, which are themselves represented by instituted corporate bodies of propositions, with the propositions in turn maintained by a corps of teachers. An initiation to the freedom to think for oneself, instruction is not the same as recruitment.

Falling in step to the cadenced rhythm arises out of a deliberate group basic training brought about in spaces of physical constraint called barracks, which have nothing of the spontaneous or involuntary about them, any more than does learning a technical skill or training within a profession. Even if it were possible to unbraid, within the complex of psychosocial propagations, the twin threads of affective dispositions (such as the Great Fear that took hold in France in 1789 or the Great Hopes of the Brazilian northeast) and logical constructs—the facts of sensibility from the facts of discourse—one would still have to discriminate, with these latter, between formations of meaning (myths, legends, and images) and statements or representations proffered as truth (scientific ideologies, for instance). So too the "belief that" of prognostication (or opinion) cannot be absorbed into the "belief *in*" of adherence to a group cause (or to a faith). What Dominique Joseph Garat called "the analysis of the understanding" in the Paris of 1800 at the time of the Ideologues, which has since that time been rechristened "cognition" in our age of software, does not suffice to make full sense of the multiple and irreducible modalities of the lifeworld of transmitted symbols.

These objections about method remain secondary vis-à-vis the objection about principle raised by genetics' promotion to explain the nongenetic. In the case of a given individual, it has proven well-nigh impossible to discern what comes under genotypal morphology and what comes under phenotypal. It has similarly been established that from the genetic legacy of a given population nothing can be inferred about its *cultural* legacy.[15] Moreover, to the cultural borders between human groups, there corresponds statistically *no* meaningful genetic map (there clearly are no hereditary diseases peculiar only to Swedish, Jewish, Arab, or Malaysian populations). On a more cultural plane, one might say that competence is innate but not performance. While our generic genetic makeup predisposes us to speech, it does not determine the tongue in which we speak. It does not induce us to write or to use ideograms versus Latin characters, or to take up the reed as scribal implement versus a keyboard. These particular variations are the stuff of technological and ethnic conditioning, precisely the two levels the naturalist approach excludes as not pertinent. Here, if we pass from method to being, we cannot keep from producing a *homo biologicus* outside society, history, and the technologies of living practices. Would not fetishizing into sole and adequate agents of transmitting cultural meanings neurochemical elements that have been uprooted from settings, affiliations, and their material memory bases amount to reducing human history to a natural history? Does it not lock away mentality within the vital, obliterating any properly social mediation between the two? Doesn't one thereby risk forgetting the Marxian maxim that man is also the world of man and that this world, which is knowledge acquired from history, is made up as much by objects and signs as by assigned social functions?

An individual's belief is not an individual phenomenon. It is a collective personality working through the individual. Whether ideological or religious, belief refers back, by its own nature, to collectivity, to a cause, obedience, or belonging. It crystallizes into orthodoxy (which is in turn an a posteriori tracing or transfer of an ortho*praxis*). To take up again the example of early Christianity, the relation of believer to God passes through a formal assembly, the *ekklesia*, that from the beginning has a territorial base, the diocese. The faithful are not called up singly by ecclesiastical *magisterium* but convened popularly by the Word of God, gathered together as one body of worshipers. Within the order of belief, the aggregate comes before the single element, and the community before the individual (here we indeed have the most basic operating mechanism and province of contagions). Biologism takes a plunge back into the individualistic explanation of the social by casting thought and memory as intraindividual processes and contagions of ideas and symbols as interindividual processes. Are behaviors (involving one's *habitus*, models of identification, idols, etc.) really the object of a contract conferring individual membership, renegotiable by each generation, from mind to mind? Our representations look to be modalities of the social ties that bind: they are inscribed in the group unconscious, invested in stereotypes (this term implying a certain stage of reproductive print technology, whence it derives), and welded to the technological and organizational mediations that clear a way for them. And their transmission cannot be likened to a mere summing of perfectly punctual conversions or to a billiard game. An individual, like humanity at large, partakes of the stuff time is made of. Dissociate him from his memories, from his technological and societal niche, and you invent something like a human plant minus soil and photosynthesis. This leaves an epidemic without pathogenic agents and favorable medium, without historical culture and immune defenses, an epidemic in which the virus propagates all by itself, by magic. It suggests the plague without rats or fleabites. And that assumes the contrived, disembodied existence of automobilistic ideas without any gearboxes, that is, apostles, patriarchs, and pilgrims; church, state, school, or party.

Shrugging off the reality of technological base and institutional relays, far from restoring the universe of symbols and mediation to its wholeness, simply makes this universe dull, by taking away its dramatic precariousness. Precisely because it is technologically conditioned, cultural transmission functions under no biochemical guarantee and remains intrinsically fragile. It cannot reap the benefits, like its biological counterpart, of a permanently active data program inscribed in DNA. *Acquired* knowledge, it is true, continuously makes headway against the *innate*, which it relieves as in a relay race to a higher level. But this second nature does not have the reproductive automatisms of living matter. What would a prehistoric representation of things have been without pictograms? We must examine the material genesis of memory—procedures for recording and modes of archiving—if we do not want to go on in a vacuum about disembodied memory, as in the psychology of faculties (or of "modules"). To reflect, for instance, on geometry and mathematics—as we have known since Husserl, whom Derrida made us read again—is to reflect on writing. One cannot speak of the same unified, timeless human memory irrespective of its having been set down in, and dependent on, a technology of letters (linear alphabetic writing in the logosphere), or analogical technologies (photography, phonography, cinematography, radiophony, etc.), or the digitized technologies of today. The substrata of transmission modify its functioning and alter the nature of its contents. To pass from one mnemotechnology to another is to change the mental horizon, the required qualification, the political community, the choice of cultural legacy, the dominant standards of learning and knowledge. A given structure of belief (and also of knowledge) changes its nature to no lesser degree in the age of technological reproduction than does the work of art itself. One cannot properly analyze a public mental representation absent its manner of publication and circulation, determined technologically and historically. This redundancy is required (history and technicity happen or disappear together).

It is supposed that the cognitive systems described by a social psychology that has been rejuvenated by the concept of information traverse historical epochs without noticeable alteration. They function in a neutral, unchanging setting; as mental equipment they have the properties of an invariant prefabrication. To this assessment one might object that in a sense there is no isolated history, either, of diseases per se, even if there is a history of man as a patient. (The two things are not the same, as Jacques Ruffié reminds us: no disease has, strictly speaking, an age in itself, only that of its duration in the host.) But then what interest can be taken in the history of religions, sciences, and art? If the development of human mores comes to nothing more than a parade of idea epidemics filing by, history loses all essentiality except as a display of clinical cases. From the moment one substitutes, on the grounds of cultural activity, Nature for History in the mythic role of *primum movens*, the current of such thinking risks redirection toward a psychology without psychic mechanisms or personality, a physiology with no technology of the body, a space without geography, a time without duration, an anthropology without paleontology, an ethnology without particular peoples, indeed the biomedical equivalent of a knife with neither blade nor handle. This is fine if we want to diminish the panoply of human civilizations to the status of a chronicle or curiosity, to mere reserves of exempla for illustrating a laboratory protocol, and if we want to invent a naked ape that would be a man, sheltered from a quantitative anthropology. Can we not fault such an imperialistic cultural genetics for excessive scientism or for not heeding the *other* sciences?

For the pangeneticists, it seems the biological individual (and not psychosocial individuality, which is not a synonym) would be the motive, inaugural, and terminal force of the cultural relation. They see in every phenomenon of social epidemic "the cumulative effect of micro-processes" (as in Dan Sperber) analogous to the "individual event" that is an illness.[16] This leads them to concentrate priority on interpersonal phenomena, linear trajectories of transmission lacking depth of time and field. There results from this a touching familialism, in the Anglo-Saxon style, of the protocols of experience; the contact/contagion is analyzed at work within the typical relations between father and child, grandfather and grandson, mother and infant, even professor and student (but without taking into account reciprocal mediations: e.g., the father-child relation as mediated by the school). It is in a psychologizing vein, the tone soon becomes moralizing, and the intention often laudable: battling against racist pseudodeterminisms and class prejudices.

Do social inequalities arise out of genetic differences? Is IQ a cause or a consequence of social status? Must academic failure be imputed to inherited traits or upbringing? By democratizing teaching, will one raise or lower the level? Is the private property of the means of production and exchange inscribed in the genome? These debates quickly become bogged down, setting ideologies and science against one another without any one having a handle on any other. The misfortune of badly posed questions is that they direct ill-formed answers. However quantified and informed the replies of those who take biology's concepts for the biology of ideas, these replies change the terrain with difficulty; they frequently keep the stamp of the socially sticky ideologies to be confronted. Can one fence off this type of polemics by opposing generosity of intention to actual values? It would not seem so. Not having been discouraged by the controversy over measures of intelligence (Binet's IQ) independent of all definition of *intelligence*, the biologizing pangeneticist school answers the sociobiologists' rapturous scientism by itself setting off in quest of measures and formulas to guarantee in similar fashion its own scientificity. Biometrics, aspiring to calculate the heritability of characters, has in this way served as a common framework for these controversies, its goal being to quantify the respective shares of innate and acquired skills within individual intelligence. To bring this off, there are some crucial experiments to observe. Will an adopted child show more correlations with its adoptive parents than with its natural ones? An even better test is to isolate the environmental coefficient and then vary it by conducting tests on identical twins raised in different households, as was done a while back with same-egg twin adults, one having been raised in East and one in West Germany. As far as we know, these in vivo experimentations have never yielded a probing and generalizable conclusion permitting some kind of prediction, and it is not hard to guess why. Measuring for one given individual the respective shares of hereditary or genotypic component and cultural or environmental component would first have to suppose that those components are (a) distinct and (b) homogeneous and thus summable. As long as they are interactive yet incommensurable, the quantitative phantasm seems destined to be dashed.

It should be clear by now why more promising fieldwork might lie elsewhere. Not that a social psychology with much to teach is to be rejected. There is, in particular, Gabriel Tarde (1843–1904), with his innovative studies of the opinion of crowds, which are more subtle and original than is suggested by textbooks' scholarly caricature of this great thinker as a monomaniacal doctrinaire of imitation. Tarde contributed in considerable measure to rid conversation, the public, the newspaper, the crowd, fashion, sects, and many other situations of what might to us seem their deceivingly obvious or anodyne comprehensibility as ready-made, influential givens.

The various psychosocial schools of thought are nonetheless burdened by what seems to me a common procedural vice: the *ab interioribus ad exteriora* method, the ease of slippage from the interior to the exterior or from individual psychic dynamics toward the collective effect. If one admits, as I do, that cultural transmission begins where interpersonal communication ends, the actual state of affairs would seem to call for the inverse method, *ab exterioribus ad interiora*. It was not Saint Thomas but Saint Paul who, never having set eyes on or heard Jesus himself, made faith in Christ *transportable*. This contagion was carried out at a distance (historically and geographically) from its point of origin. The routes of its transmission were not genetic, not reducible to familial relationships, and without crowd effects of the kind modern media entail; neither were they somnambulistically suggested, involving hypnotically induced trances in the converted. As a result, this propagation had recourse to an institution—the church—and to a determinate set of techniques for inculcating the faith (evangelism).

Mediology's change of focus attends to coordinating these two realities sui generis: the belief and the techniques. It makes its claim, if not to independence, at least to internal autonomy. And this autonomy should follow naturally, so to speak, from the principle of subsidiariness: a mediologist should treat, from his own level, so-called minor questions that major disciplines of knowledge, despite or by very reason of their superior competencies, necessarily leave pending because they are not outfitted to study them.

7

Ways of Doing

The research program implied by a mediological perspective can be divided into two branches. One side favors diachrony, asking by which networks of transmission and forms of organization a given cultural legacy was constituted. How were founding ideas themselves founded? Across which material and mental walks of life did they have to make their way? How did they negotiate and compromise with these various environments? The question can be addressed equally to great historical religions and secular ideologies, to sweeping spheres of influence and to local coteries.

On the other side, with more importance given the synchronic crosscut, the question is how the appearance of a new system or equipment modifies an institution, an established theory, or precodified practice. How does a novel technological object dislodge a traditional domain? For instance, how have successive generations of recorded imagery—at first photographic, next filmic, and finally digital—affected the adducing and administering of proof in the sciences? When the material basis of inscription, transcription, and recorded data changes, what are the repercussions for the very definition of an art? (What changes have the vinyl record and compact disc brought to music, photography to painting and to literature, etc.?) On the one hand, then, there is the geomorphology of a cultural landscape; on the other, its geodynamics.

In short, whether one surveys, so to speak, the meteor craters resulting from an unexpected object's impact on a mental planet or reconstitutes the fluidities of magma behind forming eruptive rock, it is the shock of heterogeneous elements that will interest the observer. The Catholic Church was not made to encounter the cathode ray tube and televised religion, nor were schools created for the computer, but their paths could not help crossing. As it stands, how must they make themselves over so as not to be undone by the meteorite? Culture and technology move together and cannot do without one another: the two enemy sisters do not get along but must come to a working compromise. Such compromises pass through a series of decompositions and recompositions that mark a cultural crisis, or crisis of exponential growth. And this remains the case even when it finally proves necessary to refuse the postulates and above all the melancholy attendant on these changes. (Among such refusals can be counted Plato's derisive juxtaposition of copy to original, the nostalgia for a lost mythic authenticity, and the superstition of artistic aura.) Benjamin's "The Work of Art in the Age of Mechanical Reproduction" (1936) uncontestably opened the way and established a profile for this line of inquiry. There is also his "Small History of Photography" (1931).[1] The latter calls for numerous as-yet-uncomposed complements or pendants, for example, "A Small History of the Automobile" that chronicles forms of collective consciousness in the era of individual transport as a driving force.

I recognize that my speculative profligacies and large-scale forecasts have no way of covering over the minimalist character of this proposed approach. With obstinacy and indifference to raised eyebrows, the latter places the great turning points face to face with trivial realities: a minuscule technological cause; a great civilizational impact, to use Daniel Bougnoux's juxtaposition. *Minimus curat mediologus.*[2] Indifferent to the impregnable point of view of a global conception, the angle of attack prioritizes a diminutive mediology, one that covers concrete landscapes (which are already littered with humble forgotten artifacts: the bicycle, the road, paper and pens, the candle, and the reading lamp) and case studies. Mediology's expectations turn away from the founding of a school with its garrisoned disciplinary turf and its issuing titles of nobility, its walls with arrow slits, its officer staffs, and its acknowledgments. (A university corporation has its professional interests to defend. Though hardly satisfied with disciplines that are already institutions, a mediologist, having no official roster of adherents, still has no reason to make war on those disciplines.) Even less is it a matter of some doctrine sprung fully armed from a founder's skull separating true from false and good from bad in order to cure contemporaries of their ills and illusions with subscription to a redemptive value. Why shouldn't the inquisitive researcher at work place his values between parentheses for having, like all reason's devotees, pledged fealty to the cynicism that comes with understanding? If, with mediological curiosity, one approaches frankly the modern state subject to the rule of law, republican education, living spectacle, a religious confession, or a literary genre, there still is no imperative to defend republicanism over democracy, wager

Buddha against Jesus, espouse live perception or broadcasting against deferred or taped broadcasts, or tout the novel over the epic. Why not think more in terms of an archipelagic than a fortified disciplinary space? A work in progress rather than settled system, such a semi-independent area of influence has an androgynous quality, a space that is motley with hunches. In its precincts, harlequin-hermaphrodites (to use Michel Serres's image) labor—sometimes with each other, sometimes at cross-purposes—at divergent if not contradictory interests.

Though not keen to corset with a prioris this bundle of emerging concerns, I believe something gives an undeniable family resemblance to this turn of mind shared by quite a few. Each of its hybrids finds itself incapable of letting operate, as before, the binary code of philosophical universals inherited from a past that will not stay passed (including the habits of thought it has fostered in the social sciences, where one would have least expected it to persist). This code stipulates stark bifurcations between nature and technology, spiritualism and materialism, form and substance, symbolic and material. Such antinomies can be facile and sticky; against them is set an analytical style of mixed breed, uncoercively trinitarian (that is, tirelessly seeking out the excluded third term, the medium that makes it possible to put ideas across, the carrier that makes the first term of each aforementioned antinomy pass over to the second and back). Out of negative protestation there can arise a positive mutation (as every new object that is made intelligible transforms the frames of intelligence itself).

Sometimes the moment of truth is demanded of us, as by whoever inscribed *hic Rhodus hic salta* at the foot of the wall. "So where, at long last," I may be asked, "*is* your mediology? If it is something serious, surely it has its method, does it not?" It is often typical of bodies of knowledge less certain about their foundations to fetishize methodology: they are taken up (perhaps to reassure themselves) with putting the cart before the horse. The less distinct the terrain, the harder the method: no surprise, then, that the sciences of culture and society obsess about this question more than the others do. Must I respond to the question by remarking that although studying the facts of transmission does not (yet) resort to numerical data or statistical instruments and although it cannot count on a whole century of erudite legitimations already under its belt, it sees itself poised at about the same epistemological starting place as sociology in its infancy, despite its still eccentric marginality? Like sociology, it is neither experimental nor hypothetico-deductive. And so in its turn shall it not be satisfied with establishing concrete causal connections (Weber) via a method of concommitant variations (Durkheim)? One might prefer to defend mediology as a *science humaine* by embroidering on the vast spectrum of scientist regimens already out there or wrapping oneself in a cloud of references and authorizations like the cuttlefish in its own ink. Some words of Roland Barthes might help us resist this temptation: "Sterility threatens any work that never stops proclaiming its will to method." Let it simply be enough for me to outline, in what follows, a way of going about cultivating the merest kind of skill, or knack, for mediologic practice. Three gestures in this direction—because they actually comprise a single gesture—fall unpremeditatedly into line: decentering, materializing, and dynamizing.

DECENTERING

A Chinese proverb says, "When the wise man points to the moon, the foolish one looks at the pointing finger." The mediologist shall be a fool, meticulously, and his method, a carefully argued, foolish concentration on the unexpected or the taken-for-granted. He will look thoughtfully up, down, or behind to the information's addressing system, all the more camouflaged as it is embodied. This camouflage can be found in the etymology itself of material bases and substrata: the Greek *upokeimenon* (versus the *phenomenon itself*), "not to show itself," "to be *sub-*," beneath the flotation line (like the boat's submerged keel). Hauling up to the light of day the logistics underlying the spiritual and moral realm comes under a strategy of emphasizing the opposite of what others say. But nothing short of this is called for if we want to defuse the medium's inbuilt strategy for erasing its own traces. This insistence rubs the spontaneous psychology of message producers the wrong way; mediologists are not born but made.

It is more natural and agreeable to evoke class warfare than the finer points of operation of mill trains. Critics would rather bring up an author's elaboration of metaphors than an era's techniques of manufacturing paper, narcissism than reflective surfaces, or velocity rather than the asphalt enabling it. Putting together a dictionary of works or a history of ideas gratifies readers' taste for symbolic meanings over analytical catalogs of mechanical networks, vectors, and procedures. Diderot opined in the Prospectus to the Encyclopedia that "there have been too many books written about the sciences, not a sufficient amount concerning the liberal arts, almost nothing on the mechanical arts."[3] His observation is still valuable, and—except for a few such as Diderot, Balzac, and Valéry, the French pioneers of this kind of archaeology—the great tradition has written even less about the mechanical aspects of the liberal arts. Belles lettres are an unpropitious site for the study of letters' technologic structures, as is literary theory for learning the workings of the book trade.[4] Writers treat the question "Why do you write?" as tapping a more prestigious source of activity than the vulgar question "What do you write *with?*" (types of paper, pen, or word processor; timetables; and surroundings) and more virtuous by far than a measly "On the backs of whom or what do you write?" How often do we think about the realities of nineteenth-century travel by rail, as we turn the pages of Maupassant's *Bel-Ami?* There is clear evidence, however, for a causal complex in which the popularity of journalism followed from the steel railway. Industrialized mass transport enlarged printed matter's sphere of circulation; it determined the industrialization of the press (the daily newspaper costing one sou) and brought massive influxes of money onto the intellectual scene.[5]

This shift in emphasis, from the better- to the lesser-known, can be called the mediological indexation of a phenomenon. It puts what appears marginal at the very center. It shines a light into the dead and dusty corners of literary history and the panorama of ideas. It vacates textual space or the universe of forms to take a look at contexts of carryings, makes a detour around the outside to reach the inside. This indexation proposes a reversal of the best habits picked up during one's early years at school. It inverts them by targeting atmosphere, by playing its billiards with bank shots off the cushions, and by closing in on the periphery's details as if *they* were the big picture.

Faced with a doctrine that is already constituted and presents itself as an autonomous whole, attention must be redirected from literal meaning-content to the frameworks that administer belief in that content. To do this, utterances must be subordinated to *manners of utterance* and *enunciatory instantiations.* What institution gave rise to the indoctrination and put it across? How was its doctrine propagated, inculcated, and reproduced? Which models of conformity did it follow? Like the jewel in a ring's setting or the rider atop his ride, a system of theses or ideas will have been placed in the mount of its form of collective organization. The latter will be seen to have functioned as something subject to veridical enunciation, and this enunciation in its turn to have functioned within a certain mnemotechnological complex. This complex in *its* turn served to set down, store, and circulate traces in a manner characteristic of a given, historically determined mediasphere: the logosphere, or age of orality and its first inscriptions in writing; the graphosphere, or age of print; and the videosphere of recorded images and sound, digitized and pixellated sign-pictures, and unimedia.[6]

Consider the example of the Christian religion. To index Christianity mediologically as a fait accompli of global transmission, one would have to articulate, in relation to one another: (1) a theological corpus, that is, a set of dogmas and mysteries; (2) a sacerdotal institution, that is, the pyramid of hierarchical ministries; and (3) original procedures for proclaiming, cate-chizing, and identifying, that is, such things as reading aloud the sacred text followed by an unscripted homily, a form called "scriptural proclamation" inherited from Hebraic synagogical practice.[7] These latter rituals are carri-ers of the faith, veritable tools the community has manufactured, incorpo-rating expertises originally derived from technologies of oral and lettered memory in the logosphere. Each of these three staggered stages of Christian transmission has been, though so far only separately (with a few rare excep-tions), the object of research. The doctrinal expression of the sacred is for-mulated as *theology*; cultic expression as *liturgy*; and institutional expression as *ecclesiology*. By recombining these units differently, one catches a glimpse of how much the second and third levels have acted on the first (i.e., the techniques of worship on politics and politics on symbols). The approach cuts across the methodological distributions of labor as much as the prover-bial disdain of generals for the supply corps. While the contents of Christian pronouncements were shaped by the vectors and contexts of issuance, there are now countless contemporary interpretations of the Gospel's message that give little prominence to its historical process of construction and propagation.

The mediological indexation of a political ideology such as socialism rearticulates doctrines in their juncture with institutions (schools, parties, and Internationals) and these latter in their juncture with tools (the genetic helix of school, newspaper, and book). These vertical joinings, from ideas down to materials, relativize horizontally secondary oppositions between tendencies in the mediasphere (libertarian, scientific, utopian), bringing to light the cultural technostructure that supports them all. Fratricidal quar-rels can be recognized as familial, by virtue of a common rootedness in technologies of representation now extinct. To the eyes of the warring fac-tions, the confrontations of ideas, apparatuses, and persons among different branches of the so-called worker's movement served as a kind of screen (a properly ideological one) between the actors and the global ecosystem of their action, an ecosystem that was, starkly put, movable lead type printing technology.[8] Typologues, intellectuals, and pedagogues: here were the three pillars of transmission in the universe of the proletarians. They were the flowerings of a precisely definable age in the history of media that began with Marinoni's rotary press (1850–1860), flourished especially with the Linotype typesetting machine, and came to a close with videotypesetting (1970–1980). It thus lasted approximately a century. Some estimates are that half the species that have ever lived have become extinct since the first appearance of life on earth. A good number of ideological species encounter a similar fate, at the hands of their surroundings' selective pressures (technological Darwinism is pitiless).

The idealistic postulates of this inconsistent materialism, in which a critical rationalism is synthesized precariously with a religious messianism, are no longer competitive once lettered pronouncements' techniques for analytically decomposing perceptible appearances are downgraded when those appearances are recorded by their image and sound traces on tape, film, and screen. No one will ever behold with sensory eyes an average workday or a profit margin on the TV or movie screen. The market's invisible hand has more concrete apparitions to put on exhibit in the marketplace. Every culture is an adaptive response to surroundings (Jacques Ruffié), and even if the "one species, one niche" principle does not apply mechanically in these more subtle matters, the technological niche of the videosphere proved fatal to a cultural tradition tending to put the (invisible) future before and above the (perceptible) present. The last in the line of communities of the Book, Marxists took this analytical-because-alphabetical mentality and made of it a mystique as much as a lever, offering salvation by library and literacy. In the end, however, the mystique hid from their own eyes the historical precariousness of the apparel of apparatus. Before our very eyes there has occurred a slow disintegration of that grand European mosaic of the graphosphere: publishing house dynasties, reviews, newspapers, booksellers, and readers. They had guaranteed the social viability of a bookbound culture within an ecosystem that was invisible because shared (with the internal ventilation of its pertinent oppositions). However Marxist or Proudhonian one professed to be, one did not push one's materialism to the point of identifying the actual material constituents—paper and lead—on which the grand and the small publishing houses had been founded and that melted away along with them. Political parties, movements, and splinter groups proved to be more literary than their members could ever think possible. From 1848 to 1968, encountering the masses through words on the page, the avant-garde intellectual kept up his Latin but forgot his medium.

How much thought does the myopic give to his glasses, except after misplacing them? (Can the fish discover water?) The civilization of the book is more than the circulation of printed matter. Once mother and matrix, when it recedes it takes with it the extremist aristocracy of ink and lead typesetting. Is it not by deideologizing ideologies that one can understand their appearance as well as disappearance?

More today than yesterday, one must play the fool and focus on the pointing, so as not to fall into the moon. The indexical fragment is all the more invisible because obscene, since the more present our visual media of reportorial representation, the more apparent will be the *im*mediacy, the apparent unmediatedness.[9] The more reinforced the material intermediaries of interpretation are in a given act of transmission, the more the sensation of immateriality increases. When instances of enunciation are at work, it is their strategy to the second power to reach a complete, traceless transparency at the very moment when they impose their "law."

Diderot's paradox of the comedian is reborn here as a *paradox of the interpreter*, and the name of the genial Glenn Gould merits being attached to it. The musicologist Denis Laborde has subtly taken this paradox apart and examined its workings in the case of Bach and the *Goldberg Variations*, the best-selling classical recording of all time.[10] The roughest outlines of an interpretation of the paradox would state it as the triumph of the "Gould utterance" over the "Bach utterance," were it not that the highly sophisticated orchestrating of emotion produces in us, the listeners, the effect of a quasi-ecstatic contact with an "utterance" in its purest and most untamed state, "tel qu'en Lui-même enfin" (such that he—Bach—is finally to be found truly himself), as Mallarmé's line on the entombed Poe has it.

The Gould effect can be divided into two schemes of time. The first involves the star shining his projectors on his own technique (rather than on the musical score itself), subordinating his playing to its recording sessions. The virtuoso refuses to give concerts, and his masterly execution makes a show of its emotive and pathos-filled style. The star tailors his own legend, a myth, a Gould mystique (the anorexic, the insomniac, the misanthrope, etc.). To allow the character to be fully placed in this element, the industriousness of the record making is mobilized in an elaborate mediatic deployment that truly overdoes it. At this time it could be said we no longer hear Bach done by Gould but Glenn Gould in Bach. In the second scheme of time, however, the effect is reversed. Who recalls, from then on, that the thirty-two Goldberg variations were actually composed in 1740 for two-keyboard harpsichord and not for piano? Other virtuosi interpret these variations using the instrument for which they were intended and scrupulously respect the composer's indicated tempi. These interpreters efface themselves before the utterance, and in mediatic terms they are unwise to do so: aside from the more exact and faithful rendering selling ten times less better than its re-creation, it also sounds less perfect, less true to the ear. In a second state, now carried away by the music, Gould manages to disappear as an interpreter. Like that of the illusionist carrying out a disappearing act with his own technique, the execution takes hold of us as a burst of inspiration, as if dictated in brute form, with no airs, by the original. Here seems to play the source itself, simply put to instrument: a wager won. The cumbersome question of method and interpretation yields to transparency, vibrancy, and translucency. In the end we see Gould no longer but hear Bach in person: a revelation, an encounter, a shock.

As to the plastic arts, some superbly researched treatments, like those by Michael Baxandall, Svetlana Alpers, and Nathalie Heinrich, have produced more than a classic social history of art (in, respectively, fifteenth-century Italy, sixteenth- and seventeenth-century Holland, and the age of classicism in France) by exhuming the mediations, individual or collective, internal to the art world.[11] Their method allows one to escape the eternal alternatives of sociological reductionism and tautological aestheticism. Although they do not of course use the word itself, these authors have in their own manner created a mediology *in statu nascendi* by turning attention to the side aisles and backrooms of the noble history of aesthetic canons, where, vegetating in footnotes and decidedly secondary in importance to the main lines of inquiry, labored (from the quattrocento on) indispensable individual mediators—commissioners (public and private), patrons, collectors, and dealers—as well as mediative groups or institutions—public or private academies, workshops, schools, museums, administrations, etc.—from the sixteenth and seventeenth centuries on. The intended decentering crosses things and people, grasping relations of force incorporated into produced works that can in turn modify those relations further. Thus by uncovering all that comes to intercede between an aesthete and a canvas, thereby constituting the one and the other as institutions, one dissipates the illusion of the atemporality of an ideal and inert one-on-one encounter between a subject of taste and an objet d'art. It is instead a matter of discovering what led a subject concretely to sanctify this object and said object to be exhibited behind glass or velvet ropes. For the birth of the Artist, as someone practicing a liberal profession and not just an artisanal or mechanical art, was as little spontaneous and universal an occurrence, and as intricately orchestrated, as was the birth of the Intellectual to public and symbolic prominence in the nineteenth century.

So too does mediological inquiry find kinship with a kind of knack for sniffing out contemporary creation by taking interest in everything that does not traditionally interest the aesthete or amateur: looking at the lookers, at the public and private viewings of exhibitions rather than the varnished veneer of canvases themselves; at the layout of museum rooms, with their guides and guards, their framings, wall clocks, catalog, collection curators, and recommended sequences for viewing paintings; in sum, at everything that is deployed to display and solemnize works of art. A careful study of this well-handled distraction, this periphery of cultural validation, puts us on the trail to a quite simple truth, which is not demystification but restoration of an aesthetic wholeness: art and the faith we put into it are one and the same. And there exists a technology of production of this faith, as of all others (in God, in science, or in money).

MATERIALIZING

Or, better, as François Dagognet puts it, "*re*-materializing."[12] When we view things for what they are materially, we fall back onto our feet (that is, come back to the beginning), at the risk of getting dizzy, because most of the time we walk as if with our heads, from force of habit. Our spontaneous inclination is to conceive human evolution "rather as an outpouring of the social into the material than as a two-way current whose deepest motivating factors remain material."[13] This is confirmed by the history of writing, over the course of which the nature of the inscription surface and its substance conditioned significantly the nature of the notation procedure. Civilization, insisted the historian Charles Seignobos, is roads, ports, and quays. It has become so natural to speak of culture, while forgetting civilization, that our elaborate normative displays hide from view the basic levers of interaction and negotiation with things both inert and living.

Admittedly, there may an element of self-punishment in always vexatiously redirecting values toward vectors and asserting slippery claims for the subject on the configurations of the lowly object, threadbare and mangy. Roads, ports, and quays don't sport the name of an author. Neither do the photocopier and record player. (Who remembers the name of Ferdinand von Braun and the technology laboratory of Strassburg in 1940?) Cultivated cul-

ture stands like a column covered with glorious signatures; technological culture is the poor relation, reduced to anonymous familiarities. With cultivated culture, the proper names last longer than the works; with technological
culture, the inventors are effaced behind their inventions. Fire, the wheel, and
steel were and remain signatureless, like the sewing machine. The English lad
who had been assigned to activate a crude fire engine and who, when told to
go and play, had the idea of attaching with string a tightrope balancing pole
to spigots injecting steam and water into the cylinder, advanced civilized
humanity by a giant step. His Christian name and surname (Humphrey
Potter) were not, however, part of his legacy to posterity. Every French school-
boy knows the name of Barbey d'Aurevilly; however, the bicycling enthusiast
may well be unaware of the name of the inventor of the bicycle with gear-
wheel and pinion. His invention gave us our first means of individually pow-
ered locomotion, which turned out to be, on this score, a momentous event
in the history of consciousness. We still go bicycling; we no longer read
Barbey. This fact hardly prevents us, we sophisticates of culture, from tending
assiduously to the cult of genius while relegating to nameless folklore the
inventor of the Concours Lépine. We continue to act as though inscribing a
signal on magnetic tape had nothing to do with the realm of consciousness
or how the mind works. Within the notion of *artifex* we persist in dissociat-
ing the (mechanical) artisan from the (liberal) artist. We tend to see only the
painter in the figure of Leonardo, while he saw himself as an engineer.

At the risk of overcompensation, the dangers of underinterpretation
should be preferred to the far more pervasive temptation to overinterpret
phenomena and objects, especially in the area of aesthetics. When faced
with a fixed artistic image—whether painted or sculpted, whether
Magdalenian, medieval, baroque, or avant-garde—why not lay aside the
specialized lenses of the aesthete, the semiologist, the iconologist, or the
philosopher of art? Why not disengage from style, hidden meaning, and figural codes? Instead, with deliberate naïveté, let us shift emphasis onto the
most simple-minded questions. What precisely is the material substance of
the image under consideration (how are its traces conserved)? Which material procedures produced it? What was its function? What type of attentive-
ness does it compel? Is it signed or not? Does it look to be an object that is
to remain hidden or on the contrary exhibited, touched, thrown, or carried?
Is it suited for framing, dressing up, placing under glass, or displayed in fresh
air like an everyday object? Was it considered by its manufacturers to be
beneficent, baleful, or without any physical effect on the health of its
beholder? To what universe does it give or promise access?

It will become clear, through probing of this sort, that the efficaciousness of the image as a *symbolic operation* that puts the looker into some kind of relation to something cannot be considered apart from the image's status as a *technical product,* that is, the operative chain of causes in which it is set. Let us think, for example, within the supposedly homogeneous domain of photography, about the changes of style and consciousness ushered in by the handheld camera, with its new tripodless portability, and, after that, by the Leica camera before the war. With this new piece of equipment are born instantaneousness, the scoop, atmosphere, street photography, and images taken clandestinely. Different social uses are now entailed by photography, according to whether the image is produced on a metal plate, on a negative against glass, with powder silver bromide on paper, with celluloid, with a Polaroid instant camera, or with a digital print (in this sense there are many photographies, not one). The materiality behind the camera's picture taking determines the operations of our looking.

How would a mediological angle of attack take up the history of cinema? Jean-Michel Frodon has already shown the way. The dynamic of genres is to be preferred to chronologies of auteurs; observation of films' effects and influence, to critical appreciation (labels of "good" or "bad"). One should think in terms of production and reception as much as creation, finding as much interest in the reactions of the public as in the direction of the filmmakers. Oblique connections between the technoeconomic, artistic, and social provinces of praxis can be made, but without ever forgetting what distinguishes the cinematographic phenomenon, as a mechanical device and attendant set of practices, from its elder and younger brothers, the theater and television: being a process of *projection* different from theatrical spectacle and televisual broadcasting.[14] It is of capital importance to a mediologist how films are viewed (collectively in hushed darkness, with tickets bought at the door), how movie houses are laid out (from Rex to multiplex), and what kinds of ceremonies and contextual emphases put the industry across (posters, film festivals, Oscars, appreciations, publicity, etc.), all purely circumstantial trifles in the eyes of the cinephile. He gives thought to such things as the abandonment of the turning reel of perforated, unexposed negative within the classic film camera—moving at twenty-four frames per second, a kind of skin highly sensitive to the flesh of the world—in favor of the digital image. Along with the editing table's replacement by computer editing (which permits a different reconstruction of the illusion of duration), he wonders how such changes are going to modify the very texture of films and human feelings. All such technical details will have their effects beyond special effects, in particular on the dispersal of publics, on the social imagination, and on the narrative structure of films, as well as on their communication modes (broken up into projection in theaters and video and television watching at home).[15]

A day might come, in the still-far-off future, when the shift in weighting relative research priorities that mediology recommends will end up as a slippage too far to the other side of the horse. This will happen if and when it attains the state of self-sufficient giddiness (or the hubris mentioned earlier) into which holders of a would-be explanatory master key sometimes fall. As we pass from the book as text to the book as object, the history of the book could risk erasing that of literature. The crudeness of materialist underinterpreting would at this point form the pendant to the snobbish overrefinement of our Hellenistic overinterpretations. Overvaluing the code and undervaluing the channel was yesterday's semiocratic indulgence. Stopping before getting to the referent, the mediocrat might succumb to the opposite realist fallacy: overestimating the channel at the code's expense. To each his own penchant, as long as the effort climbs an upward slope.

DYNAMIZING

Restoring to logistics their central role is not enough. If the notion of a vehicle has heuristic value, underlining the centrality of the *medium* (that which occupies the middle) will serve to highlight the efficient dynamism of the *mediate* (that through which one thing relates to another). Analyzing mediations in practice relegates the observational (the inventory of places) to the performative, involving an inventory of metamorphoses (of everything that crosses through these places). Grasping discourse as a course, a journey across and a distance covered, and substituting an anatomy of vectors for an exegesis of values oblige us to break with an empiricism in the Anglo-Saxon mold. Consider, as illustration, the historical example of eighteenth-century France's passage from Enlightenment to Revolution.

It is not without interest to juxtapose here two original specialists of intellectual history, both valuable in their own right. Both ask themselves the same question, how were the ideas of 1789 transmitted? And both set out from the same refusal to apply the old saw, "it was Voltaire's fault, it was Rousseau's fault," which is a tautology that explains nothing. The first specialist is our contemporary, Robert Darnton; the second an ancestor,

Auguste Cochin (1877–1926). Here reappear, at a high level of excellence, versions of the American and European lines I considered in the first chapter. In an outstanding article, Darnton proposes to pass "from the history of the book to the history of communication."[16] Historians of ideas (such as Daniel Mornet) having tended to concentrate on textual analysis, those who take up sociocultural history have, in place of that, turned more recently to the history of the book. Darnton (and others of course) want to leave the confines of both the book and the narrow bounds of "the 'idea' as a unit of thought or an autonomous vehicle of meaning." Because meaning does not inhere automatically in ideas (as Wittgenstein showed), it becomes necessary to move from the history of ideas to that of meaning if we want to take into account the broad spectrum of all flows of information that can circulate, in both directions, between the man in the street and the Great Author, taking such forms as pamphlets, rumors, songs, common reports, tracts, lampoons, caricatures, word of mouth, leaflets, and satires. One needs to produce a complex schematic outline of flows that joins such media to the corresponding places and spheres of activity that diffuse them: the court, salons, marketplaces, cafes, public gardens, booksellers, and libraries. Oral transmission and written communication are relayed through these crossings, the first amplifying the second. So, the sphere of ideas has happily been broadened, but the entirety of the process is still conceived in terms of *communication*: the force of ideas lies in how widely they are spread.

Auguste Cochin conceived the movement of the Enlightenment in terms of *community*.[17] His binoculars were set on the role of the *sociétés*—lodges, philosophical societies, clubs, and factions—showing everything that was implicated in the transition from literary salon to philosophical society. The latter proved to be an original kind of social organization (and, for our author, one that was against the norm) of men who came together on an equal footing, not linked by heredity or experience but exclusively by ideas and free will to participate. The nature of these associations suggested, without any need to thematize it, that a theoretical refounding of society on the large scale was a viable possibility. Out of this came the capital formation, richer and thus less known than "the medium is the message," that "method engenders doctrine." The force of ideas resides in how their carriers are organized. And the socialization of thoughts finds its truest line of force in the politicization of those who, socializing those thoughts, compose a certain type of society. The word *communication* is nowhere pronounced by this Catholic Chartist, and neither is *media*, yet a (republican) mediologist, even as he aspires to combine the two approaches, will feel theoretically closer to Cochin the militant monarchist than to Darnton the enlightened democrat.

The observation can be extended to sites of sociability, the linchpins of that area of activity between the private sphere and the domain of the state that is today called "public space." More than relays, these sites function as matrices: their frequenter does not emerge in the same state he was in before becoming part of them (they are more than mechanical carriers like buses or mailboxes). Eighteenth-century salons engendered a certain literature and narrative structure, with such genres as the dialogue, the epigram, and the digressive or picaresque narrative. The process was analogous to the way in which Parisian cafés at the beginning of the nineteenth century, more than simple way stations or meeting places, informed modes of public discussion, a certain journalistic style, and a distinctive class consciousness. Need it be recalled yet again that the philosophical discussions of our cafés is not the philosophy taught in a high school classroom, just as a play for the enclosed theater in the Italian style is not the same as a play written for performance at Avignon (or as the tabloid newspaper's layout gives rise to far different features from those of a format like that of *Le Monde*)? One sees that the abstract notion of public space is not operational in its present form if it is not connected with the workings of any recognizable technocultural systems in movement. *Space* is something that projects *into time*: it is molded on the nature of *dynamic networks* (the contemporary cybercafé). Being vectors of highly individualized transmission, the salon, the stage, or the classroom do not yield up for indifferent consumption just anything, like some vending machine of values and ideas. Without overlooking that grade school directs students toward an atemporal ethic of truth, for example, and that staging a play procures irreplaceable, unrepeatable impressions of concrete presence, the mediological eye must be trained to perceive, in any walk of life as in any form of media, more than simple means for spreading ready-made ideas or data: those means are veritable agents of *transformation* of the given content.

Whoever would relate a link whose nature is that of a symbol or sign to an instrumental linchpin will ipso facto be led to a diachronic approach, one that puts the substantial forms of the repertory into movement again. Mediological indexation is necessarily historicizing and sensitive to the genesis of ideas and forms in their contexts. Even if culture is the residue left when one has forgotten completely about the techniques and technologies that produced it, putting these indexations in full view can have its demystifying virtues. It detotemizes the functions of seemingly disembodied or now-contextless symbols by uncovering the organization whose function they once served.

Take, for example, the "holy office" of the French Intellectual, a truism of sociologies of culture and our own truism as well, by ricochet.[18] It is finally from neither the force of clarity of their ideas nor their personal articulateness (insufficient if sometimes necessary virtues) that the so-called great intellectuals (those men or women of study who shuttle from personal library to public forum) derive their social efficacy. They derive it from *the means put in their hands to publish, appear in public, and participate in debate.* They partake of the influence, or heavenly mana, that their apparatus of diffusion lends them. This apparatus is a delegation that passes unnoticed or is even denied by many of their contemporaries (because of the relative lack of inside knowledge about the workings of organs of influence). We tend instead to ascribe its effects spontaneously to the intellectuals themselves. The indexation needs to reimmerse these high priests in their professional milieu (the clerisy of its day) and then this milieu in the optimal medium that structures it. The type of praxis (in this case, intellectual) or one subject's influence on another is illumined by the *techne* of vectors of influence: putting in place a new material base of inscription and recording amounts to tearing down and setting up a new authority, every new age favoring the subverters of the dominant material base. The manuscriptural base of the scriptorium (organized materiality), which was behind the order of the clerisy (materialized organization) constituted by monasteries and universities, gave rise to copyists and illuminators (at the same time that the royal court and market towns were fostering the writing of poems and chansons de geste in the vernacular). The printing press generated printers and engravers, those pillars of the circles of literate lay humanists. Radio waves widened the circle of notoriety, creating new reputations for people from civil society and the professions (doctors, singers, and actors) who took over the baton from credentialed intellectuals (writers, professors, and scientists) in the relay race to transmit. They proved to have a broader impact when it comes to the oratorical, functional niche of moral criticism and opinion making.

Each logistical change is translated by a change of operative machinery. One cannot therefore speak of *the* Intellectual but of a succession and interlocking, or englobing, of one cultural system by (within) another. The intelligentsia is organized by its mnemotechnological devices, and the logic of the organizing delivers over the evolutionary logic of the habitat.[19]

One should similarly avoid speaking about the unitary object of art-historical study as *the* Image (as did the classic philosopher) but rather about visual artifacts over their long history. Again and again, a new dynamics of material base and processes of crafting or producing renews the pragmatics of representing, that is, the recipe for creating that answers the question, "What purpose does this image serve for me?" Elsewhere I have traced the history of Western art through three heterogeneous phases of functional images: the idol, or magico-religious, regime; the art regime (a highly transitory, localized stage); and the visual regime (of electronically and digitally reproduced imagery).[20] There is no possible overlap among the primitive idol as an *aid to surviving death* (a tool for those without tools), the art image as an *aid to pleasure*, and the technological image as an *aid to knowledge* (or as information). The intermediary functions of images evolve at the crossroads of our belief systems and our mechanical outfittings. Their distinct evolutions brightly bear witness to the more subterranean mutations of our culture. What common alignments can there possibly be among successive superimpositions of the *magical* gaze of an onlooker for whom the (two- or three-dimensional) image is a living being, opening access to the supernatural, to God or the Cosmos; *aesthetic* or disinterested contemplation, whose purpose is solitary pleasure, private delectation; and the contemporary distracted glance one can associate with *utilitarian* or *economic* purposes? Scouting out products, controlling technical operations, identifying consumer goods—all at a distance and often directed by the pressures of saving time (which dictate the semiotic efficiency of such things as logos, designer labels, brand names, and videos)—all of this falls within the regime of the "visual" (Serge Daney's term) when the production of an image of the world no longer corresponds to a lived experience of this world.

Telling the history of almost anything, more than setting up a chronology, means proposing a sound periodization, at the risk of schematizing more than is necessary. When one carves up a continuum based on overlayered generations of materials, taken in the broad sense, the segments can be distinguished as so many mediaspheres, the principal sociotechnological systems of transmission that have followed one another, with some overlap and achronological tangling, since the invention of writing: secondary orality, printed word, and audiovisuality. These currents also constituted once-durable structures like architectural frameworks, infrastructures, or reinforcement, global technological coherences (by virtue of their devices' systematic interdependencies) on the inside of which each cultural walk of life expends prodigious effort constructing its own architecture in the style it is bequeathed by its own history and geography. My tripartite segmentation into logosphere, graphosphere, and videosphere is obviously rudimentary and incomplete. It gives a knowing Hegelian wink to the holy trinity by leaving out crucial phases at either end: the originary mnemosphere of primary oralities (practiced by societies without writing) and the further conversion of visuality in the videosphere to a numerosphere (with its technology for the electronic digital compression of signals). One is readily tempted too, when it comes to fine-dating a cultural instant, by Ferdinand Braudel's well-known overleaved temporalities. To overlay our own divisions with his, our mediasphere, the ecological and indivisible time of macrosystems of transmission, is analogous to Braudel's geographic time; the more atmospheric but already perceptible time of spheres of influence, sensibilities, or pervasive trends (baroque, classical, modern, etc.) is analogous to his social time; and the time of schools and works, with its short rhythm, is analogous to the brief spasms of his eventful time. Still, the model needs to be tempered by remembering, first, that the mediaspheres are not set up in perfect sequences like dominoes but can over- and underlap each other at points in the strata, like the intricate foliations of a puffed pastry, and, second, that there is a latency period for technological breakthroughs. Take the examples of writing and printing by press. Until about 1550, argues Paul Zumthor, these two technologies were more collaborative than at cross-purposes. And actually the full effects of print technology would not become apparent until the nineteenth century, owing to obligatory popular education, which would make of printed words a writing for the masses. Here we see what Jacques Perriault's study of communication machines, *La logique de l'usage*, calls the "coach-style effect" that makes innovation enter the future backward. The first wagons of railcars were basically horse-drawn coaches on rail, just as the first printed pages took the form of manuscripts, the first photographs looked like still lifes, the first moving pictures suggested theatrical plays, the first automobiles resembled horseless horse-drawn vehicles, and the television in 1955 was a radio cabinet that emitted images along with sounds. Every moment of technological actuality is late for its own party.

Third, the Braudelian model should be nuanced by remembering the *critical* character of the transitions. Even if in the long view these transitions appear simply to accumulate rather than supplant one another, in the short term each leg of their aggregate journey was rocky. The replacement of incorporated memory through its objectivization in more sophisticated textual preservation around the sixth century in Greece or the substitution of a dead memory for a living one—that is, of papyrus scroll for recitation by *aoidos* or rhapsode—was lived as a catastrophe (at least in Plato's eyes). And yet what a leap was made by written text, endowing signs with a new capacity to act at a distance, outside the author's presence. All the prodigious things that are being similarly brought about nowadays by the leap of objectivized memory to industrialized memory that take us so aback and renew us—events such as intimate sufferings, undue relegations, national humiliations, corporate lockouts, and struggles for survival—can be measured day after day by absolutely everyone, each in his minuscule sphere of personal life.

A DISCIPLINARY PROVISO

To whoever imputes to me a too holistic or totalizing ambition, I can reply that my intention is not to say *everything* about the mechanisms of mediation. Or to set the red cherry of a doctrine triumphantly atop the cake of empirical research, which would be ridiculous, impossible to do, and idle. It is instead perhaps simply to pronounce some near nothings apropos just about everything (that constitutes culture). In this manner I have sought, by separate treatments elsewhere, to trace a few steps toward a *political* mediology of the state, socialism, or the nation; toward an *aesthetic* mediology by examining the conditions that gave birth to art; toward a *religious* mediology of the Christian religion; and toward a *representational* mediology of theater and spectacle.[21] This parti pris can also direct efforts toward better understanding the workings of such activities as organized sports, psychoanalysis, geography, and of course even mediology itself. The angle of view would have the same thematic: how does the mediated object of study transmit itself and its meanings, and how, by transmitting itself, is it constituted? The educated wager is that by tugging on the thread of the *how*, a good portion of the *why* can also be unraveled. The initial guiding thread may be slight, inadequate, or partial yet also a crucial part of the weave. The approach is far from exhausting its potential objects, though there might well be, in the case of the hard sciences in particular, a rather limited interest. If it is true that the universality of scientific knowledge is the end result of a manufacturing process that is social and technological, indeed political, contentious, and laborious—experiments needing to be replicated, articles accepted and published in reviews recognized as authoritative, colleagues convinced, caps feathered, labs commandeered—a scientific result nonetheless transcends *in fine* the codified conditions of its utterance. Once sent into the particular orbit of renown, the issued statement of findings will turn all by itself, that is, within the gravitational field of the paradigm currently in force.

The mediological disposition cannot really stand in place of other dimensions that it is suitable to find infinitely worthier of reflection, not only in the sciences but in art and religion. Perhaps we will not sidestep the risk of understanding less and explaining more when we can understand better and explain less. We must be wary of claiming to utter the law, essence, or best of things. And yet a genealogy from below still seems to me to encircle in a useful way objects as otherwise far afield of mass media as Byzantine icons or photography, the republic or parliamentary monarchy, the clergy or Freemasonry. I ask, with the tireless ill-spiritedness of very misplaced questioning, "Where do you come from?" "What places have you passed through?" "How do you refer to yourself and present yourself to others?" *Unde, qua, quomodo*: Where, what, how? You there, beautiful aesthetic form, majestic political institution, noble domain of competencies, state, nation, artwork, international association, scientific discipline, literary genre, religious confession: What compromises enabled you to become an institution? On which supporting materials, machineries, and networks does your survival depend? Permit me for an instant to suspend my judgment, bracket your message and ends, your perfections and truths, your salvational values, so that I may consider simply your comings and goings, your vectors and vehicles, the living stuff that conferred on you living form and without which you would never have arrived here among us.

AGAINST THE STREAM

The aspect of every age goes through cycles, and the age that we seem to be entering portends contrariness in the face of such impertinent pertinences. It is the right time to persuade ourselves that mediologic materialism without stoicism can only mean the shipwreck of the soul. Yesterday, following the avant-gardes of researchers and *littérateurs* (via Saussure and, especially for we French, structuralism), the City of Culture as a whole tuned its instruments to the paradigm of Language. Having passed out of fashion, the latter is yielding pride of place, via the cognitive sciences, to a new philosophy of mind. Yet from the linguistic turn to the cognitivist one, the road's surface has hardly altered, and even the cargo is very similar. We can detect this in the same suppleness of the stringing together of arguments, in the ease of reconversions. As far as can be judged by humors and murmurs, the future does not promise, for the type of inquiries whose profiles have been awkwardly sketched here, better academic, mediatic, and social fortune than has the immediate past.

"How the waves of language swell high," that felicitous early prophet Wittgenstein, exclaimed once upon a time. Indeed, and even though Lévi-Strauss, from within the field that concerned him, repeatedly recommended to the servants of the Signifier that they immerse themselves in the every-day reality of tools and techniques (so that they might get to know that *about which* things were being said), the rising crest of the linguistic model contributed in no small measure to consigning the materialities of culture to the subordinate far reaches. The unconscious, political economy, play, fashion, love, history, and nature itself were structured "like a language." The reduction of Homo sapiens to *Homo loquens* found epistemological author-ization in advances that had been made in the sciences of language and pub-licly in the unprecedented immersion of the human species in a gigantic ocean of words and phrases (Hagège). Hence the credibility, from above and below, of a world in which everything was reduced to its sign.

And that was how the rejection of the established order by the pioneers of a new analytical model took on the force of orthodoxy in the space of about thirty years. While groundbreaking study of prehistoric man was dis-covering the crucial correlation of facial and manual polarities in the devel-opment of hominids and, more vastly, the bidimensionality of saying and doing, those whose job it became to enlighten opinion on the matter were giving to language an autocratic autonomy. In the era of omnipresent signi-fiers, the human organism most in prominence *dwindled to his apparatus of phonation*. Knowledge was reduced to plays of language; history to a sequence of grand narratives; philosophy to a hermeneutics; and our most humble practices all became languages or grammars. Human action itself was labeled "communicational." And when public space had been upgraded to a norm and reference with the new democrats, it was understood as the space in which an ideal language situation (Habermas) makes possible the universalization of interests. In the examination of logics of action by those paradoxically most audaciously hostile to intellectualism, legitimacy and its principles shunted such questions as material efficacy and its constraints to the margins. At the same moment that the most meritorious sociology was dematerializing relations of force and mechanisms of domination, the best literary criticism was immolating the uses of things in their "signification," typewriters in "the space of the text," and the book's bookhood as object and commodity in "intertextuality." Leading-edge political science was turning its interest to symbolic violence and not real war or the historical evolutions of armaments, to exam booklets more than to the operation of police commissions, to hierarchies of symbols more than of, say, university degrees, military rank, orders, or legal jurisdiction. All this time, reflection about religion was producing a New Testament without a church, while the logic of economic theory was substituting services for material production.

In a word, the day was won not for culture's epidermises, skeletons, and underpinnings but for thinking about thought. "And for a very good reason," the Marxist will retort, "if in fact Big Science has become a productive force, if companies cling to their 'incorporeal assets,' if financial immaterialism is winning out over the totality of economic acts. Nothing truly important takes place out of step with the times; it is the very course of things and history that has accredited and spread the new logocracy." One understands how, amid the general artificial levitation, imprisoning spirit in signs should have seemed like a widening of intellectual possibilities. It is fathomable too that semiological reductionism went to the point of making the industrial object one more sign among others, as if giving attention to material (and neomaterial) things would divert one from meaning and as if adding actual performances to significations made for a zero-sum game.

At the same time, the inflation of language as a growing denial of our increasing technological embeddedness permitted a flourishing sociology whose analysis of the everyday was subjective, aestheticizing, and full of stylistic sparkle and neologism. It cultivated these qualities at the expense of experimental patience, the establishment of facts, and the correlations that joined them together. When it did confront what it took to be the irresistible or ineluctable, it enthroned some idlenesses that were more or less poorly thought through. There was the exorcistic use of Heideggerian *Gestell* (whereby technology's bill of health was declared to be poor), a sacramental formula relieving one of the need to make actual inquiries into historical matters.[22]

Also present were the old scholarly duel between pure science versus applied science, latent under repeated devaluations of the technosciences; the scant consideration that the cultural world gave to genealogists of the technological phenomenon (when they were not actually playing inquisitor to and excommunicating it), as well as the almost nonexistent place it reserved for the history of technology within the subjects studied in higher education; the disdain of authorized history of science for that of industrial science, patents, and laboratories; the primacy accorded any doctrine founded on denigration or minimization of machineries (from phenomenology to semiology, in academia, or from New Age prophecy to the situationists' denunciation of "spectacle" among French journalistic circles); and the relegation of objects, materials, media, and cultural artifacts to the back-row seats of university orthodoxy.[23]

Those who did develop an attentive, informed criticism of technological filiations and breaks, from Bertrand Gille to Georges Simondon, were confined to a good deal of intellectual isolation. This was not only due to elitism of the speculative theorists or to the literary learned's aristocratic condescension. Nor was it simply the price paid for running counter to the *sensus communis* (there being no more economical ploy to gain public approval than by denouncing technology's dictatorship and taking up the religious discourse of the Fall in the name of nature, soul, lived experience, and lost origins or human will). More than all this, with the denegation of material mediations we are paying for a long ancestral heritage of neglect. It goes back, as far as we inheritors of Greek habits of thinking are concerned, to a primordial partition by now so well absorbed into the very substance of our thought that it seems natural and self-evident. Must I recall, after so many others, the genealogy of this grand initial mental block, overdetermined as it was by such an extraordinary confluence of reasons internal to system? One reason was of course economic, stemming from the slave system and overabundance of available labor. Another was social, having to do with the antinomy of manual labor and studious leisure, the servile versus the contemplative life. A third reason was theological, given that *physis* as primal motive power was looked on as sacred, which made *techne* an impious counterfeiting of the divine. And a fourth was scientific, a result of the epistemological impossibility of the noble mind's ever reflecting on the sublunary world's nonmathematicizable approximations, making unthinkable such things as glasses, telescopes, or precise chronometers.[24] Aristotelian vitalism put the finishing touches on this restrictive consistency by separating living beings, who contain within them the principle of their own movement, from inanimate objects deprived of all dynamism proper. Against matter is thus set spirit, as against the slave the citizen and against the mechanical arts the liberal arts, regardless of water clocks, sundials, and catapults.

Heavy and insistent is the suppression that weighs on our spontaneous technophobia. We must relearn every day to jettison its ballast if we want to reclaim the great wide open of heterogeneous nonhuman things outside ourselves, to get away from the mind's *chez-soi*. We need to extend the freedom of the anthropological city to those nonhuman things (so much have we, since the time of the Greeks, ranked technological fact habitually beneath political right). This would be one way of resisting an inculpatory philosophical terrorism that consists in putting the onus of proof on an area of inquiry deemed a priori incapable of using the very terms and values by which it has been prejudged since Plato. It is today taken for granted, with all the force of authoritative argument lending its weight, that it is no longer up to speculative philosophy to account for its own blindness to technological instrumentation but rather up to technology to exonerate itself daily of philosophy's charges. As to those who judge it the most pressing issue of our day to reflect on thought's *unthought* materialities, much of contemporary philosophy would have them go take a draught of their own shame.

So the difficulty should not be underestimated. Studying transmissions as an object unto itself creates a problem of disciplinary classification that, given the *ratio studiorum* currently in force, has no solution in the short term. (And in the long term we're all dead.) It is characteristic of research that proceeds "diagonally" (as Roger Caillois terms it), or what we presently refer to as interdisciplines, to disrupt what the established order of study has taken so much trouble to order conveniently. One hundred years from now, the blueprints of a twenty-first-century museum of science and technology might show some stray corner devoted to a virtual and perfected mediology, with spaces allotted here for the *cognitive* sciences, or sciences of mind, elsewhere for the *objective* (experimental or exact) sciences, and finally one for the *accreditive* sciences that would be those of society (history, economics, sociology, and religious and political sciences). Phenomena of *belief*, on which collective life rests, are the least understood of all. And if we already know very little about how we know, we know still less about how we *believe*. Bringing to light the industries of believing and inculcating belief, through an examination of the processes that constitute authority and the infrastructures of credibility, might contribute in the future to consolidating this less-explored third encyclopedic sector. Its objects would be marked out in conjunction with, and behind, other fully accredited and licensed undertakings.

As things stand now, these transversal defectors will be accused of fishing in unquiet or turgid waters, and with reason: disturbed orders are their very object. There is disturbance when one body alters something of another body.[25] Owing to the fact that interiority intermingles and interacts with material and mechanized exteriority (Dagognet), machines and entities are unflaggingly parasitical on one another. The person seeking to make these fruitful pollutions intelligible will inevitably be seized with a professional or disciplinary disquiet. (Still taken with purism and even more so devoted to its own security, the immemorial idealism continues to dissociate spirit from things.) When standard repertories are infiltrated, traditional domains intermixed, the "sublime" knocked down a peg or two by the "trivial," such catastrophes destabilize intellectual categories, insular comforts, and turfs. The impure hodgepodge of interests and ways of seeing condemns one to a dual exile. Techies will send the dreamer to the likes of philosophers, who will in turn refer this sort of intellectual plumber to the other proles of Mind. Mediologic ambition is a bit too earthy and historical to cajole a *philosophia perennis* devoted to the empirico-transcendental division of mental labor (try talking about papyrus and codices to an exegete of Plotinus and Descartes or puckishly asking a Lacanian what to do with the "mirror stage" before mirrors were invented). Mediological ambition is also too fervent about religion, art, and the immobilization of time to call on information and communication sciences so disdainful of the antique (bring up the subject of angels to a sociologist of reception or the myth of Thoth to a specialist of cable plans). Mediology refrains from pledging fealty to one or the other academic compartmentalization, from identifying with one or the other political ideology. And it lacks a beautiful moral cause to defend (other than getting at the truth of the matter, an inadequate hook) or social grievance to redress (other than an interest in knowledge without immediate ulterior interests). As such, it stands to undergo a rather long purgatory, between a lost home in the university and an improbable refuge.

All this is but par for the course: every Long March begins with a banishment. Dwellers at the border and migrants might even profit from their period in NFA ("No Fixed Abode") status, which after all has its leisures, to assess carefully the epistemological obstacles thrown up every time one upsets established customs elevated to certitudes. The mediological undertaking would indeed seem a megalomaniac's whim, rather than an attempt at gaining reflexive knowledge, were it not for its relentless interrogation of its own weaknesses, rendering modesty obligatory (though it has that anyway). Instructed in the ways and phenomena of authorization, exclusion, slides into oblivion, and loss, it is no more badly placed than the next profession for understanding that the least infringement on the orchestral score as written will inevitably (and happily) elicit protest and resistance.[26]

It pays to appreciate, in their full force, both the best and the worst reasons the prevailing canons will have to belittle or banalize this anti-discipline. Among the better reasons is the understandably disliked raid on professional gains by the oblivious and hurried philistine. The guardians of the established human sciences do indeed have something to resent, because they know all too well what requisites and laborious delays inhere in the creation of autonomous fields of expertise. Chief among these rules of method figures the indispensable break with the uncritical notions of common consciousness, notions that continue to swell up on the periphery and rise to assail the abstractions that have been won through noble warfare by the entrenched institution. Among the worst reasons should be counted a too categorical defensiveness of niche or turf or of corporativist interests that are by nature precarious and under threat (accreditations, awards committees, readerships and audiences, echoes, and other honors). Hence the hypersensitivity of the most well-established networks of Reason to everything that makes forays into the surrounding area of the security perimeter, as any prowler may be a potential predator or seducer.

Let me add for the record the self-regard of intellectual bosses who, having let their names and renown be identified with a given, officially recognized position, have a certain tendency to liken the controversy of arguments and theories to a conflict of people, that is, a struggle over places and influence between people. These and so many other inevitable or justified grievances can be made. But I do not wish to cry foul: the milieu's mean-spiritedness is consubstantial with it. It is a fact of Nature and of mediological nature. Thus has operated transmission, within the universe of knowledge as in the others, ever since there has been doctrine, with the same inextricable interarticulation of professional ethical concerns and sudden bursts of zoological evolution. It is here one perceives the limits of the metaphor of assigning things their proper place, confined as it is to the notion of *having* and to ordered slots, whereas the spread of ideas has to do with causes and territories, that is, with the very *being* of knowledge.

These, then, are necessary sidestreet excursions that can be foreseen and are even semireassuring. They obviously will not impede anyone, on a quite cantonal scale, from deriving some manic encouragement from the young Hegel's conclusion that if reality is inconceivable, we must forge inconceivable concepts. The work of disenchantment is endless, fortunately. An eternal power, tutelary and deified, our Mother Nature long ago found herself segmented, at the time of and after the profaners of the Renaissance, into the disjointed series of physico-mathematical phenomena. Next, in place of the humors, forces and mysterious designs that since antiquity had fetishized life, experimental biology came to substitute matter, particles, and laws (François Jacob). How are we not to doubt that a day will come when Culture, with its terrifying capital letter and stepmotherly smothering, will be supplanted by some incongruous methods of analysis putting in her place technology, environmental/social contexts, and functional needs? If the laborers in mediology, with their rudimentary tools and meager means, hasten on that day, however little, they will not have lived and sought to transmit in vain.

NOTES

[All translations are mine, unless otherwise indicated. Wherever possible, French texts cited in the original are followed by citations, within square brackets, of English translations. Translator's notes are set off in square brackets and followed by the abbreviation "Trans."—Trans.]

1. THE MEDIUM'S TWO BODIES

1. One can contrast this enterprise of constructed duration with post- or premodern declarations of precariousness and transience, apotheosized in the happenings of the 1960s. Let us recall, however, that even Hinduism and Buddhism's consecration of impermanence is taken to give entry to the atemporal. And though Navajo sand paintings, which so fascinate contemporary tastes, are designed to be erased, the shaman's elect training in the execution of an ephemeral work still presupposes the transmission of a know-how, that is, a collective victory over the ephemeral.

2. [The sociologist Rodney Stark undertakes just such an inquiry into the networks of transmission of early Christianity. See his *Rise of Christianity: How the Obscure, Marginal Jesus Movement Became the Dominant Religious Force in the Western World in a Few Centuries* (San Francisco: HarperCollins, 1997). In a sense, Stark goes in the reverse direction, by using source material and statistics on contemporary cult activities to better reconstruct the new faith's plausible routes of transmission in the first few centuries A.D. But the same mutual insights into past and present to which Debray refers apply in this study.—Trans.]

3. [The classic elaborations are by Pierre Bourdieu. See his "Cultural Reproduction and Social Reproduction," in J. Karabel and A. H. Halsey, *Power and Ideology in Education* (New York: Oxford University Press, 1977): 451–487; and his *Reproduction in Education, Society and Culture*, 2d ed. (London: Sage, 1990).—Trans.]

4. [Debray avows his debt in this area to a growing body of scholarship tracing the history of libraries and literature as an official, popular, or pedagogical institution. Pertinent overviews in English include Roger Chartier, *The Order of Books:*

Readers, Authors, and Libraries in Europe Between the Fourteenth and Eighteenth Centuries, trans. Lydia Cochrane (Stanford: Stanford University Press, 1994); Robert Escarpit, *Sociology of Literature* (London: Cass, 1971); Robert Darnton, "Reading, Writing, and Publishing in Eighteenth-Century France: A Case-Study in the Sociology of Literature," *Daedalus* 100, no. 1 (1971): 214–256; idem, "What Is the History of Books?" *Daedalus* 3, no. 3 (1982): 65–83; idem, "First Steps Toward a History of Reading," *Australian Journal of French Studies* 23, no. 1 (January–April 1986): 5–30; idem, "Toward a History of Reading," *Wilson Quarterly* 13, no. 4 (1989): 86–102; and Lionel Gossman's essays "Literature in Education," "The Figaros of Literature," and "History and Literature: Reproduction or Signification," chs. 2, 3, and 7 in his *Between History and Literature* (Cambridge: Harvard University Press, 1990).—Trans.]

5. Jean-Luc Piveteau, *Temps du territoire* (Geneva: Zoé, 1995).

6. ["SPEUSIPPUS (b. circa 407, d. 339 B.C.), Athenian philosopher, son of Eurymedon and of Plato's sister Potone. He accompanied Plato on his last visit to Sicily (361) and succeeded him as head of the Academy from 347 to 339. Of his voluminous writings only fragments and later reports remain, but Aristotle treats him with respect and it is clear that he continued and helped to shape some major philosophical interests which the Academy had acquired under Plato." (Gwilym Owen, entry in *The Oxford Classical Dictionary,* 2d ed., ed. N. G. L. Hammond and H. H. Scullard [Oxford: Oxford University Press, 1970]).—Trans.]

7. ["XENOCRATES of Chalcedon, son of Agathenor, disciple of Plato and head of the Academy from 339 to 314 B.C. POLEMON of Athens, head of the Academy from the death of Xenocrates (314–313 B.C.), who converted him from a dissolute life and whose zealous follower he was, to his own death in 270, when he was succeeded by his pupil Crates." (Guy Cromwell Field and William David Ross, in ibid.—Trans.]

2. CROSSROADS OR DOUBLE HELIX?

1. [Historical spadework of the kind Debray's approach champions is not lacking. There is sociological inquiry into the genesis of technical systems, as well as technical inquiry into social ones, though it is arguable that one or the other focus tends to dominate in one or the other kind of research. Of the former, there is especially the work of sociology of scientific and technical knowledge, as in Steven Shapin and Simon Shaffer, Bruno Latour and David Bloor, David Landes and Otto Mayr, but much of their work, which oscillates sharply between the documented details of case histories of empirical science and more sweeping theoretical pronouncements, is laudable more in its reconstructive detail and as monographs of social constructivism in scientific knowledge rather than of daily life in its concrete material-technological determinations. To cite stray examples more in this latter vein (whatever it may lack of theoretical or mediological self-consciousness), Georges Vigarello traces the history of cleanliness and plumbing as a social institution in *Le propre et le sale:*

L'hygiène du corps depuis le moyen âge (Paris: Seuil, 1985). Benson Bobrick offers a social history of city transport with *Labyrinths of Iron: Subways in History, Myth, Art, Technology, and War* (New York: Holt, 1981). Margaret and Robert Hazen's *Keepers of the Flame: The Role of Fire in American Culture, 1775–1925* (Princeton: Princeton University Press, 1992) documents the social organization of heating and flame. Wolfgang Schivelbusch does much the same thing for urban and rural lighting in *Disenchanted Night: The Industrialization of Light in the Nineteenth Century* (Berkeley: University of California Press, 1995) and for railway travel in *The Railway Journey: The Industrialization of Time and Space in the Nineteenth Century* (Berkeley: University of California Press, 1990). Catherine Bertho-Lavenir has edited an institutional study of *L'histoire des Télécommunications en France* (Paris: Erès, 1984) (see also n. 4, below). Thomas P. Hughes takes up electrification in Western society (1880–1930) in his *Networks of Power* (Baltimore: Johns Hopkins University Press, 1983). And the development of astronautics appears as a sociopolitical and cultural phenomenon in Howard McCurdy's *Space and the American Imagination* (Washington, D.C.: Smithsonian University Press, 1997) and Peter Redfield's "Beneath a Modern Sky: Space Technology and Its Place on the Ground," *Science, Technology, and Human Values* 21, no. 3 (summer 1996): 251–274. A thorough (and brief) overview of the professional impact that the U.S. history of technology and media has had on a generation of French historians is traced by Catherine Bertho-Lavenir in her "Clio médiologue," *Les Cahiers de médiologie*, no. 6 (2d semester 1988): 106–114. While these studies pass for something we might vaguely term "material history," they also flesh out the historical component of a mediological approach, to the degree that machines in these cases constitute the very medium, or ecology, in which new social groupings adapt, commune, suffer, and the like, vis-à-vis the technological world. For similar monographs on the material history of painting, see Debray's remarks in ch. 7.—Trans.]

2. Emile Benveniste, *Le vocabulaire des institutions indo-européennes* (Paris: Minuit, 1969), vol. 2, ch. 7 [*Indo-European Language and Society*, trans. Elizabeth Palmer (Coral Gables: University of Miami Press, 1973)]

3. [By "angelism," Debray seems to be referring simply to the reduction of the actual material mechanics of message bearing to the nonessentiality of an instrument (in the sense of a mere means to an end), alongside the respective determinate political realisms with which it is paired. The term in French typically betokens a disposition to believe oneself discarnate, to behave in the manner of pure spirit. For more on medieval angelology, however, as a once heavily freighted code for the hierarchies and dynamics of transmitting messages and doctrine, see ch. 3.—Trans.]

4. Frédéric Barbier and Catherine Bertho-Lavenir have observed this guiding principle of historical inquiry admirably with respect to the last two centuries (from the ancien régime's library collections to Japanese video) in their *Histoire des médias: de Diderot à Internet* (Paris: Armand Collin, 1996).

5. ["Truly, truly, I say to you, unless a grain of wheat falls into the earth and dies,

it remains alone; but if it dies, it bears much fruit. He who loves his life loses it, and he who hates his life in this world will keep it for the eternal life" (John 12:24–25).—Trans.]

6. A. Berman, "Traduction, communication, entropie," presentation at the colloquium "Mémoire du futur," 1985.

7. Charles Péguy, "Note sur M. Bergson et la philosophie bergsonienne," in *Oeuvres en prose* (Paris: Gallimard, 1992), 3:1273.

3. THE EXACT SCIENCE OF ANGELS

1. [This translation is slightly modified from A. Poulin, *"Duino Elegies" and "The Sonnets to Orpheus"* (Boston: Houghton Mifflin, 1977), p. 13.—Trans.]

2. ["Let no one disqualify you, insisting on self-abasement and worship of angels, taking his stand on visions, puffed up without reason by his sensuous mind, and not holding fast to the Head, for whom the whole body, nourished and knit together through its joints and ligaments, grows with a growth that is from God" (Colossians 2:18–19).—Trans.]

3. [This unknown late-fifth-century author of mystical texts on angels was for a long time erroneously conflated with a Dionysius the Areopagite mentioned in The Acts 17:34. By the middle ninth century, both were also confused with the bishop Dionysius or Denys (Denis) who had been sent to Gaul by Pope Clement I in 250 and was martyred in 258(?), along with a priest, Rusticus, and deacon, Eleutherius, on present-day Montmartre (occasioning the legend of the beheaded saint carrying his own head to burial at the site of the église Saint Denis).—Trans.]

4. [For a more elaborate genealogy of the metaphysics of light and solar radiation as the basis of "mediologically naive" models of classical Reason, see especially Régis Debray, *Media Manifestos: On the Technological Transmission of Cultural Forms,* trans. Eric Rauth (London: Verso, 1996), pp. 81–86. Thomas Kuhn offered a condensed textual history of Neoplatonic sun worship, addressing its philosophical pertinence to Copernicus's and Kepler's heliocentrism, in *The Copernican Revolution: Planetary Astronomy in the Development of Western Thought* (Cambridge: Harvard University Press, 1957), pp. 129–133.—Trans.]

5. The royalist character of the church and the clerical character of the royal court mirror one another. In the French Republic the president still has his "House" (the official appellation of the staff of the presidential palace). And the ceremonials of democratic life are as suffused with precedents and the according of status, and ministerial councils as obsessed with quarrels over formalities, as in the old Merovingian rituals or Saint-Simon's memoirs. While the *order* of protocol may change, the protocol itself endures. Observing formalities is doubtless what is deepest in political existence; so too does it withstand all changes in regime, latitude, and vocabulary. Men must be separated by rituals to keep them from slaughtering each other, a truth Sartre considered self-evident.

6. *L'univers dionysien: Structure hiérarchique du monde selon le pseudo-Denys* (Paris: Aubier, 1954), p. 104.

7. [See Serres's Diderot-like dialogue about angels between Pia and Pantope in his *Angels: A Modern Myth*, trans. Francis Cowper (Paris: Flammarion, 1995). A (similarly dialogic) overview of Serres's work, a good portion of it by now translated into English, can be found in Michel Serres, with Bruno Latour, *Conversations on Science, Culture, and Time*, trans. Roxanne Lapidus (Ann Arbor: University of Michigan Press, 1995).—Trans.]

8. [*Plato's Symposium; or, The Drinking Party*, trans. Michael Joyce (originally published in London by Everyman's Library in 1935), in *The Collected Dialogues of Plato*, ed. Edith Hamilton and Huntington Cairns (Princeton: Princeton University Press, 1961), p. 555, 202e.—Trans.]

4. FAULT LINES

1. [See especially, in English, Tzvetan Todorov's meditation on Columbus and the *conquista* in a founding text of "Cultural Studies," *The Conquest of America: The Question of the Other*, trans. Richard Howard (New York: HarperCollins, 1984 [original published in 1982]).—Trans.]

2. [Lucien Febvre and Henri-Jean Martin, *The Coming of the Book: The Impact of Printing, 1450–1800*, trans. David Gerard (London: Verso, 1990 [original published in 1958]), pp. 20–24.—Trans.]

3. Nor is this tendency in contradiction with archaic technological stages occupying the same territorial space. Virtually Paleolithic practices in parts of Australia and Neolithic ones in Venezuela can still be found, but they are a survival of the past, marginal anachronisms in the process of being assimilated (with whatever resistance) precisely because of the universality and uniformity toward which the most recent technical systems tend.

5. TOOL LINES

1. Emile-August Chartier ("Alain"), *Propos* (Paris: Gallimard, 1920), p. 60.

2. On the origins and foundations of reticulation, one can profitably consult Daniel Parrochia's *Philosophie des réseaux* (Paris: Presses Universitaires de France, 1993), André Guillerme's noteworthy articles (in association with the Ponts et Chaussés), and the research presentations collected under the title *Réseaux et territoires: Significations croisées*, published by L'Aube in 1996 and edited by Jean-Marc Offner and Denise Pumain.

3. [In the Anglo-American context, one notable instance of this disciplinary drift is the work of Benedict Anderson, a professor of international studies who incorporates strong doses of comparative ethnography into his study of nationalisms in colonial and postcolonial history. To point out, additionally, the attraction exerted

by ethnological writing on more properly literary studies of modernity in English may be to belabor the obvious, but surely the names and work of Jameson, Eagleton, Torgovnick, and Cheyfitz come to mind, with an especially balanced, global-historical exemplar to be found in Michael Valdez Moses' *The Novel and the Globalization of Culture* (New York: Oxford University Press, 1995).—Trans.]

4. [François Dagognet's books have not been translated into English. A useful, if brief, introduction in English to his thought and work on epistemology, the sciences and medicine, the aesthetics of perception, and the philosophy of material culture can be found in his "Regional Epistemology with Possibilities for Expansion," *Science in Context* 9, no. 1 (spring 1996): 5–16.—Trans.]

5. Michel Melot, ed., *Nouvelles Alexandries: Les grands chantiers de bibliothèques dans le monde* (Paris: Cercle de la Librairie, 1996), p. 3.

6. [For multiple perspectives on the formation and changing significance of roadways throughout French and European history, see the topical issue titled "Qu'est-ce qu'une route?" ed. François Dagognet, *Les Cahiers de médiologie*, no. 2 (2d semester 1996).—Trans.]

7. Claude Hagège, *Le souffle de la langue* (Paris: Odile Jacob, 1990).

8. André Leroi-Gourhan, *Le geste et la parole*, vol. 2, *La mémoire et les rythmes* (Paris: Albin Michel, 1970), p. 190.

9. My *Critique of Political Reason* (London: Verso, 1983 [original published in 1981]) contains a more detailed analysis of this mechanism in terms of the constancy principle; see pp. 323–345.

10. [*Discourse on the Origin and Foundations of Inequality Among Men*, trans. Roger D. Masters and Judith K. Masters, in Jean-Jacques Rousseau, *The First and Second Discourses*, ed. Roger D. Masters (New York: St. Martin's Press, 1964), pp. 114–115.—Trans.]

11. Blaise Pascal, *Fragment d'un traité du vide* (1647) in *Pensées et opuscules*, ed. Léon Brunchvicg (Paris: Hachette, 1912), p. 80.

12. *Etudes d'histoire et de philosophie des sciences* (Paris: Vrin, 1979), p. 362. [An introduction in English to the work of this epistemologist of physiology and biology is George Canguilhem, *A Vital Rationalist: Selected Writings*, ed. François Delaporte, trans. Arthur Goldhammer (New York: Zone, 1994). Two other of Canguilhem's studies appeared earlier in English as *Ideology and Rationality*, trans. Arthur Goldhammer (Cambridge, Mass.: MIT Press, 1988), and *The Normal and the Pathological*, trans. Carolyn Fawcet (New York: Zone, 1989).—Trans.]

13. Karl Marx, *The Eighteenth Brumaire of Louis Bonaparte*, in *The Marx-Engels Reader*, ed. Robert C. Tucker (New York: Norton, 1972), p. 437.

14. See elaborations on this by Jean Clair, *Theimer: Notes pour un parcours* (Prague, 1996).

15. Sea and air routes have no solid substrata, it might be objected, but they do become materialized by numbers and lines on maps and navigation charts, a material memory source that *is* tangible and storable.

16. [In contrast to "sociobiology," which he defines "as the systematic study of the biological basis of all forms of behavior, in all kinds of organisms, including man," Edward O. Wilson gives a helpful summation of ethology, as "the study of whole patterns of behavior or organisms under natural conditions. Ethology was pioneered by Julian Huxley, Karl von Frisch, Konrad Lorenz, Nikolaas Tinbergen, and a few others and is now being pursued by a large new generation of innovative and productive investigators. It has remained most concerned with the particularity of the behavior patterns shown by each species, the ways these patterns adapt animals to the special challenges of their environments, and the steps by which one pattern gives rise to another as the species themselves undergo genetic evolution. Increasingly, modern ethology is being linked to studies of the nervous system and the effects of hormones on behavior. Its investigators have become deeply involved with developmental processes and even learning, formerly the nearly exclusive domain of psychology, and they have begun to include man among the species most closely scrutinized. The emphasis of ethology remains on the individual organism and the physiology of organisms" (*On Human Nature* [Cambridge: Harvard University Press: 1978], p. 16).—Trans.]

17. [Marcel Mauss, "Techniques of the Body," in *Incorporations*, ed. Jonathan Crary and Sanford Kwinter (Cambridge, Mass.: MIT Press, 1992), p. 461.—Trans.]

18. The major works of André Leroi-Gourhan (1912–1986) are *Evolution et techniques*, vol. 1, *L'homme et la matière* (Paris: Albin Michel, Sciences d'aujourd'hui, 1943), vol. 2, *Milieu et techniques* (Paris: Albin Michel, Sciences d'aujourd'hui, 1945), and, above all, his masterwork *Le geste et la parole*, vol. 1, *Techniques et langage* (1964; reprint, Paris: Albin Michel, 1974), and vol. 2, *La mémoire et les rythmes* (1965; reprint, Paris: Albin Michel, 1970). [See, in English, André Leroi-Gourhan, *Gesture and Speech*, trans. Anna Bostock Berger, intro. Randall White (Cambridge, Mass.: MIT Press, 1993) and "Birth and Early Development of Technology," chs. 1–3 in Maurice Daumas, ed. *A History of Technology and Invention: Progress Through the Ages*, vol. 1., *The Origins of Technological Civilization*, trans. Eileen B. Hennessy (New York: Crown, 1969), pp. 12–76. A complete, twenty-one-page bibliography of the works, as well as an extensive interview with the author, can be found in A. Leroi-Gourhan, *Les racines du monde: Entretiens avec Claude-Henri Rocquet* (Paris: Belfond, 1982).—Trans.]

19. *La technique et le temps*, vol. 1, *La faute d'Epiméthée* (Paris: Galilée, 1994) [*Technics and Time*, vol. 1, *The Fault of Epimetheus*, trans. Richard Beardsworth and George Collins (Stanford: Stanford University Press, 1998)] and vol. 2, *La désorientation* (Paris: Galilée, 1996). [So far untranslated into English.—Trans.]

6. DISCIPLINARY IMPERIALISMS

1. Georges Canguilhem, *La connaissance de la vie* (Paris: Vrin, 1975), p. 129. [This sentence of Canguilhem's does not appear in English among the several extracts

from the second edition of *La connaissance de la vie* (1989) translated in *A Vital Rationalist: Selected Writings from Georges Canguilhem*, ed. Françis Delaporte, trans. Arthur Goldhammer (New York: Zone, 1994).—Trans.]

2. André Leroi-Gourhan, *Le geste et la parole*, vol. 1, *Technique et langage* (1964; reprint, Paris: Albin Michel, 1974), p. 212.

3. André Leroi-Gourhan, *Le geste et la parole*, vol. 2, *La mémoire et les rythmes* (1965; reprint, Paris: Albin Michel, 1970), pp. 198 and 259.

4. A rigorous analysis of this process can be found in Alain Gras, Sophie Gras, and L. Poirot-Delpêche, *Grandeur et dépendance: Sociologie des macrosystèmes techniques* (Paris: Presses Universitaires de France, 1993).

5. [Rather than "direct object," Debray actually uses the term *le complément d'objet*. Grammatical taxonomy parses the model sentence into subject and predicate, with the complement decomposing the latter further into "an added word or expression by which a predication is made complete" (*Merriam Webster's Collegiate Dictionary*, 10th ed.) as in "They made Saul *king*." In French grammatical terminology, the part of the predicate other than the verb is called the *complément* and takes on all the varieties of parts of speech, such as *complément d'objet direct*, *complément d'objet indirect*, *complément du nom*, *du prénom*, *de l'adjectif*, *de l'adverbe*, and so forth (as in "C'est une lettre de Marie," where *de Marie* is the [possessive] complement of the noun *lettre*, or in "Ton propos est contraire à mes habitudes," where *habitudes* is the complement of the adjective *contraire*). Since the complement of a subject and verb in a sentence supplies a semantic deficiency by completing their elaboration in the rest of the sentence, one might think of it as analogous in this way to the prosthetic device of technology vis-à-vis will or intentionality in Debray's and Stiegler's scheme of things. The use of analogy with semantics and grammar would imply a commensurateness between the unfolding of a sentence and the unfolding of actions by which subjects using tools clarify their own nature through the interaction. But nothing of such commensurateness is proposed or pursued systematically. Debray is of course at opposite ends philosophically from the British logical positivists, who start from the sentence as a picture of the world of things and actions, which world, in turn, confirms or refutes the case of each proposition, or word picture. For Debray, tool use precedes and undergirds philosophical propositionalism and the analytic school that practiced it. By Debray's lights, it might instead be more interesting to historicize such strains as logical positivism itself, by asking whether the state of technologies of transmission in the environment can be associated, even if dialectically, with the philosophical movement. For example, did Bloomsbury, or Russell, Whitehead, and Wittgenstein, define their thinking in opposition to technological appropriations? How was their modernism linked more subtly to its context of technology and tools of mediation? What did Bertrand Russell, or Wittgenstein, or A. J. Ayer have to say about trains and telephones? Friedrich A. Kittler attempts something of this line of inquiry, for German romanticism and Nietzsche, in his *Discourse Networks, 1800/1900* (Stanford: Stanford University Press,

1990). Robert Brain pursues it, for the material history of linguistics, in his "Standards and Semiotics," in *Inscribing Science: Scientific Texts and the Materiality of Communication*, ed. Timothy Lenoir (Stanford: Stanford University Press, 1998), pp. 249–284.—Trans.]

6. "A kind of revelation came to me in the hospital. I was ill in New York. I wondered where I had seen girls walking the way my nurses walked. I had the time to think about it. At last I realized that it was in movies. Returning to France, I noticed how common this gait was, especially in Paris; the girls were French and they too were walking in this way. In fact, American walking fashions had begun to arrive over here, thanks to the movies. This was an idea I could generalize" (Marcel Mauss, "Techniques of the Body," in *Incorporations*, ed. Jonathan Crary and Sanford Kwinter [Cambridge, Mass.: MIT Press, 1992], p. 461).

7. As Bernard Lahire notably points out in his "Pratiques d'écriture et sens pratique," in *Identité, lecture, écriture*.

8. Thus Philippe Corcuff's work, which relies on the categories of Jack Goody. In the course of an inquiry into organized labor, Corcuff notices that the opposition between professional sociology and the sociology of social actors makes the same divisions as the opposition *written* versus *oral*. In his linking of the hazier categories belonging to actors below to the flow of speech and his connecting the strict hierarchy of notions characteristic of interpreters from on high to their training within written culture, this sociologist is led to make an entirely understandable incursion on mediological terrain.

9. Habermas appears to take up this Hellenic duality by minimalizing a singularly conceived technology to a purely procedural set of factors shorn of all obligation of an axiological nature. Technical tasks, he says, could therefore be resolved in a purely administrative fashion. See his *La technique et la science comme idéologie* (Paris: Gallimard, 1973).

10. [*On Television*, trans. Priscilla Parkhurst Ferguson (New York: New Press, 1998). Bourdieu's book, published in France as *Sur la télévision* (Paris: Liber, 1996), was based on two television lectures he gave from the Collège de France. A counterpart in the context of the U.K., though a bit more dated and more sympathetic to TV as a popular medium, is Raymond William's *Television: Technology and Cultural Form*, originally published in 1974 (Hanover: Wesleyan University Press, 1992).—Trans.]

11. M. Feldman and L. Cavalli-Sforza, *Cultural Transmission and Evolution: A Quantitative Approach* (Princeton: Princeton University Press, 1981). See also Luca Cavalli-Sforza's *Gènes, peuples et langues* (Paris: Odile Jacob, 1996).

12. *Une épistémologie de l'espace concret* (Paris: Vrin, 1977), ch. 4 ("Cartographie et psychologie"), p. 169.

13. Dan Sperber, *Explaining Culture: A Naturalistic Approach* (Oxford: Blackwell, 1996). [A response to Sperber's work by Debray appeared as a commentary in *The Times Literary Supplement*, July 4, 1997, pp. 14–15, titled "A Plague Without Fleabites."

It was an early version of arguments reworked into the text of this second part of the chapter.—Trans.]

14. Emmanuel Todd, *The Explanation of Ideology: Family Structures and Social Systems*, trans. David Garrioch (Oxford: Basil Blackwell, 1985) [originally published in French, as *Le destin des immigrés: Assimilation et ségrégation dans les démocraties occidentales* (Paris: Seuil, 1994)].

15. See Maurice Olender, ed., "La transmission," *Le genre humain*, no. 3–4 (1982).

16. [Dan Sperber, *Explaining Culture: A Naturalistic Approach* (Oxford: Blackwell, 1996), p. 2.—Trans.]

7. WAYS OF DOING

1. [For the latter essay, see W. Benjamin, *"One-Way Street" and Other Writings*, trans. Edmund Jephcott and Kingsley Shorter (London: New Left, 1979), pp. 240–257. The former is included in W. Benjamin, *Illuminations*, trans. Harry Zohn (New York: Schocken, 1969), pp. 217–251. Debray himself offers a short philosophical sketch of the "photographic revolution," in its unanticipated relations to state power, in the first chapter of his *L'état séducteur: Les révolutions médiologiques du pouvoir* (Paris: Gallimard, 1993), pp. 17–62.—Trans.]

2. For a list of decisive insignificances of methodological interest, see particularly my *Cours de médiologie générale* (Paris: Gallimard, 1991), p. 35.

3. [Stephen J. Gendzier, trans. and ed., *Denis Diderot's The Encyclopedia: Selections* (New York: Harper and Row, 1967), p. 38. Published in 1750, Diderot's prospectus was incorporated into his "Preliminary Discourse" to the *Encyclopedia* in 1751.—Trans.]

4. [Scholars whose early training was in literary theory (for example, structuralist) and in literary history have nevertheless recently taken a more mediological path. Four noteworthy contributions in their respective areas are Maurice Couturier's *Textual Communication: A Print-Based Theory of the Novel* (London: Routledge, 1991); Martyn Lyons's *Le Triomphe du livre: Une histoire sociologique de la lecture dans la France du XIXe siècle* (Paris: Promodis, 1987) (though the title page of this rich work notes "traduit de l'anglais," no original version in English seems to have been published); Lennard J. Davis's *Factual Fictions: The Origins of the English Novel* (Philadelphia: University of Pennsylvania Press, 1996); and Adrian Johns, *The Nature of the Book: Print and Knowledge in the Making* (Chicago: University of Chicago Press, 1998.—Trans.]

5. Siegfried Kracauer, *Jacques Offenbach; ou, Le secret du Second Empire* (Paris: Le Promeneur, 1994).

6. [For a further elaboration of these roughly chronological epochs of representation, especially in their relation to changing regimes of belief in the visible products of (mythologized) technologies, see R. Debray, "The Three Ages of Looking," *Critical Inquiry* 21 (spring 1995): 529–555. For a genealogy of the effects of represen-

tational and inscriptive technologies on the Word, see R. Debray, *Le scribe* (Paris: Grasset, 1980).—Trans.]

7. I allude here to the noteworthy works of Maurice Sachot on Christian antiquity. See particularly *Les chrétiens et leurs doctrines: Manuel de théologie* (Strasbourg: Centre d'Etudes et de Recherches Interdiciplinaires en Théologie [CERIT, Desclée], 1987).

8. For a more detailed analysis, see my *Cours de médiologie générale* (Paris: Gallimard, 1991), ninth lesson ("Vie et mort d'un écosystème: *Le socialisme*"). [In English, a whirlwind critique of Marxism's reluctance to think through fully its own implication in a mediasphere of transmission ("Nothing less materialist, on balance, than this philosophical materialism") can be found in R. Debray, *Media Manifestos: On the Technological Transmission of Cultural Forms*, trans. Eric Rauth (London: Verso, 1996), pp. 88–97.—Trans.]

9. [Debray borrows his notion of the "pointing" "indexical fragment," or "index" (*indice*) from the U.S. philosopher Charles S. Peirce's writings on semiotics. In a paper Peirce delivered to the American Academy of Arts and Sciences in 1867, he defined three kinds of representations: "symbols," "likenesses" or "icons," and "indices." "Those [representations]," Peirce declared, "the ground of whose relation to their objects is an imputed character, which are the same as *general signs*, . . . may be termed *Symbols*. . . . Those whose relation to their object is a mere community in some quality . . . may be termed *Likenesses*. . . . Those whose relation to their objects consists in a correspondence in fact . . . may be termed *Indices*" ("On a New List of Categories," *Writings of Charles S. Peirce: A Chronological Edition*, ed. Edward C. Moore, Max H. Fisch, Christian J. W. Kloesel, Don D. Roberts, and Lynn A. Ziegler, vol. 2, *1867–1871* [Bloomington: Indiana University Press, 1982], p. 56). Later refinements of these insights led to understanding the *index* as some remaining fragment of the object or contiguity with it causally, such that the part points toward, and is taken for, the whole, as in the case of relic for saint, footprint for traveler, or smoke for fire. The *icon*, or likeness, resembled the object but was not strictly speaking *of* it, except by the less direct analogy of proportion or form, as in a picture (an artistic work). The *symbol*'s relation to the object was the most purely conventional, arbitrary and indispensably deciphered as a code.

Debray has argued elsewhere (see "The Three Ages of Looking," in *Vie et mort de l'image: Une histoire du regard en Occident* [Paris: Gallimard, Collection Folio/Essais, 1992]; and *L'état séducteur*) that the most pervasive and compelling mode of representation in our visibility-oriented videosphere of ocular and positivist credulity is now *indexical*. (The age of the *icon*, "Art," is past; the era of the *symbol* or *sign* depends on instant recognitions, more and more given over to simplified picture signs with messages about utility, class, ideology, etc., flatly signaled, such as by "icons"—an archaism—on the computer screen.) Reading *indices* relies on recognizing the essential relation of immediate *causation* between the object and the referent that is videotic, photographic, televisual, radiophonic, sound-recorded, filmic, or pixellated based on photography or some kind of camera technology that digitizes the *trace of the real object* imaged.

This monotonous reliance on video-documented realia, though it itself has its conventions, editings, and doctorings, produces in modern consciousness a priority on the immediate, the factually positive, the reportable, and the graphic. Paradoxically, however, because of its equation with the real itself, we as viewers accede to such representation being basically all there is *for the moment*, being the positive, eye-evidentiary, doubting-Thomas bottom line of an event's truth, going *beyond* the critical margin of skepticism or minimal disbelief that Lionel Trilling seemed to have in mind when he wrote, "It is characteristic of the intellectual life of our culture that it fosters a form of *assent* which does not involve actual *credence*" (*Sincerity and Authenticity* [Cambridge: Harvard University Press, 1972], p. 171; my italics). Call this visicredulity "CNN authenticity." But the paradox is: the more *material* our standards of video verification, the more *immaterial* our ties to the origins, sources, and causes of mechanically and multiply reproduced visual traces. Representations have become so pervasively mediate that they seem *im*mediate to everyone who can "experience" them at once and yet so immediate (in the indexical directness of the trace's relation to its unquestionable source) that experience itself becomes indirect, placing greater emphasis on superficial and abstract consciousness of positive contexts mediating it than on the raw datum itself. (Debray, later in this chapter: "The regime of the 'visual' . . . when the production of an image of the world doesn't correspond to a lived experience of this world.")

The dilemma may well be how an understanding of the materiality of media itself can avoid becoming yet another mediated abstraction. One might address this problem by saying that a lot depends on *how* and *where* you put your point across, and this *how* and *where* are what Debray urges us to scrutinize critically.—Trans.]

10. Denis Laborde, "Un service public de l'émotion musicale," *Gradhiva*, no. 17 (1995). This is a remarkable treatment of the subject, a must-read.

11. See Antoine Hennion's interpretation, "De l'étude des médias à l'analyse de la médiation: Esquisse d'une problématique," *Média-pouvoirs*, no. 20 (October–December 1990).

12. F. Dagognet, *Rematérialiser, matières, et matérialisme* (Paris: Vrin, 1989).

13. A. Leroi-Gourhan, *Le geste et la parole: Techniques et langage* (1964; reprint, Paris: Albin Michel, 1974), p. 210. Additionally, "Things stand in such a way that we are more familiar with the most prestigiously prominent relations of exchange than with everyday exchanges, with high-profile ritual performances than with banal exchanges, with the circulation of dowry wealth than with the circulation of vegetables—in short, we know the *thought* of societies much better than their 'body' " (ibid.).

14. See J.-M. Frodon, *L'âge moderne du cinéma français: De la Nouvelle Vague à nos jours* (Paris: Flammarion, 1995), particularly the prologue (a short discourse on an uncertain method).

15. One might also wish to consult the mediological perspectives on the theater as a material medium collected as "La querelle du spectacle" in *Les cahiers de médiologie*, no. 1 (1st semester 1996). [For Debray's historical situating of Guy Debord's likening of rampant consumerist ocularcentrism and dramatization to "spectacle," see R. Debray, "A Few Remarks Apropos the 'Spectacle,' " in *Towards a Theory of the Image*, ed. Jon Thompson (Maastricht: Jan van Eyck Akademie, 1996), pp. 64–74.—Trans.]

16. "La France, ton café fout le camp," *Actes de la recherche en sciences sociales*, no. 100 (December 1993): 16–26.

17. A. Cochin, *La Révolution et la libre pensée* (Paris: Plon, 1923).

18. [One of the most encompassing treatments in English of this historical and cultural institution remains Priscilla Parkhurst Clark's *Literary France: The Making of a Culture* (Berkeley: University of California Press, 1987), especially ch. 7, "The Writer as Intellectual Hero," pp. 159–191. It can be read as a transatlantic pendant to historical treatments in both Debray's *Teachers, Intellectual, Celebrities: The Intellectuals of Modern France*, trans. David Macey (London: Verso, 1981), and his *L'état séducteur.*—Trans.]

19. A detailed development of these consequences for the historical evolution of the French intelligentsia (1880–1979) can be found in my *Teachers, Writers, Celebrities*.

20. [Debray is alluding to his *Vie et mort de l'image*. Chapter 8 has been translated into English as "The Three Ages of Looking" (see n. 6, above). Parts of chapter 2 appeared in English as "The Image vs. Language: Transmitting Symbols," trans. Eric Rauth, *Common Knowledge* 4, no. 2 (fall 1995), pp. 51–69. A translation of parts of chs. 5 and 9 was published under the title "The Myth of Art" in *ViceVersa*, no. 49 (July–September 1995): 30–34.—Trans.]

21. [For Debray's foray in political mediology, see especially *L'état séducteur*; *Critique of Political Reason*, trans. David Macey (London: Verso, 1983); and *Le Scribe*. The mediological history of images (of which Art makes up a relatively short phase) can be found in *Vie et mort de l'image* and "The Three Ages of Looking." A treatment of Christianity's bases in media of transmission and their theology appears in "Le mystère de l'Incarnation" and "L'expérimentation chrétienne" in *Cours de médiologie générale*, pp. 89–192. And a reexamination of theatrical and spectacular representation and their historical transformations is the subject of articles in "La querelle du spectacle" in *Les Cahiers de médiologie.*—Trans.]

22. [The pertinent essay here is Heidegger's "Die Frage nach der Technik," in Martin Heidegger, *Vorträge und Aufsätze* (Pfullingen: Neske, 1954), pp. 13–40, translated into English by William Lovitt as *"The Question Concerning Technology" and Other Essays* (San Francisco: Harper and Row, 1977).—Trans.]

23. It should be pointed out that our most illustrious students of technology were not trained to the specifications of the great alma mater of liberal higher education. In France, only heterodox thinkers from other professions seem to make their mark

in those climes of academe (Haudricourt the Agronomist, Leroi-Gourhan the Autodidact, Dagognet the Doctor). Such are the heavy costs of producing actual field knowledge independently of the prior prescriptive epistemologies or ample methodological considerations so fostered by the faculties of humanities and human sciences.

24. See Pierre-Maxime Schuhl, *Machinisme et philosophie* (Paris: Alcan, 1938). [On the kinds of clocks that *were* invented and used ingeniously by the ancients, see especially Daniel Boorstin, "Measuring the Dark Hours," book 1, ch. 4, in *The Discoverers* (New York: Random House, 1985), pp. 26–33.—Trans.]

25. F. Dagognet, *Le trouble* (Lyon: Les Empêcheurs de penser en rond, 1994).

26. Many objective environmental pressures influence cultural selection. Among them must be counted the differences of notoriety, at a given place and moment, among the putative founding fathers of spheres of influence who share the same habitat. To locate oneself, however wrongly or misguidedly, somewhere on the intellectual family tree of Leroi-Gourhan rather than that of Lévi-Strauss is indisputably a comparative handicap in the jockeyings for consideration. Invoking tutelarily the latter figure (fully deserving of the admiration he is accorded) will arouse the interest of knowledgeable publics from New York to Tokyo to Moscow to Buenos Aires. References to the former, who is unclassifiable (Bergsonian or Marxist? Spiritualist or materialist?) and not well-known (translated belatedly, if hardly at all) will fall into a sort of black hole before those same audiences, a real perplexity for whoever wants to take credit for being influenced by his work. Yet Leroi-Gourhan and Lévi-Strauss were contemporaries, colleagues, and friends. The fact that the thought of the one has not spread while that of the other has met with worldwide success constitutes a notable mediological case in itself. It is almost as worthy of examination, mutatis mutandis, as the comparable fates one hundred years ago of the systems of Auguste Comte and Karl Marx.

BIBLIOGRAPHY

[English translations are in brackets, beneath the French title.—Trans.]

Arendt, Hannah. *La crise de la culture*. Paris: Folio, 1989.

[——. *Between Past and Future*. New York: Penguin, 1961.]

Barbier, Frédéric and Catherine Berthot-Lavenir. *Histoire des médias: De Diderot à Internet*. Paris: Armand Colin, 1996.

Beaune, Jean-Claude. *La technologie introuvable*. Paris: Vrin, 1980.

Benjamin, Walter. *Ecrits français*. Paris: Gallimard, 1991.

Benveniste, Emile. *Le vocabulaire des institutions indo-européennes*. Paris: Minuit, 1969.

[——. *Indo-European Language and Society*. Trans. Elizabeth Palmer. Coral Gables: University of Miami Press, 1973.]

Berque, Augustin. *Médiance: De milieux en paysage*. Gap: Reclus, Géographiques, 1991.

Bougnoux, Daniel. *Sciences de l'information et de la communication*. Paris: Larousse, 1994

Bourdieu, Pierre and Jean-Claude Passeron. *La Reproduction*. Paris: Minuit, 1970.

[——. *Reproduction in Education, Society and Culture*. 2d ed. London: Sage, 1990.]

Bourdieu, Pierre. "Stratégies de reproduction et transmission des pouvoirs." *Actes de la recherche en sciences sociales*, no. 105 (1994).

Breton, Philippe. *A l'image de l'homme: Du golem aux créatures virtuelles*. Paris: Seuil, 1995.

Calvez, J.-Y., L. Hamon, and L. Moulin. *Formation et défense des "orthodoxies" dans les eglises et les groupements d'inspiration politique*. Colloque de Namur. Namur: Faculté Notre-Dame, 1987.

Canguilhem, Georges. *La connaissance de la vie*. Paris: Vrin, 1975.

[——. *A Vital Rationalist: Selected Writings*. Trans. Arthur Goldhammer. New York: Zone, 1994.]

——. *Etudes d'histoire et de philosophie des sciences*. Paris: Vrin, 1979.

——. *Idéologie et rationalité dans la vie*. Paris: Vrin, 1975.

[——. *Ideology and Rationality*. Trans. Arthur Goldhammer. Cambridge, Mass.: MIT Press, 1988.]

Cavalli-Sforza, Luca. *Gènes, peuples, et langues*. Paris: Odile Jacob, 1996.

Chartier, Roger. *L'ordre des livres: Lecteurs, auteurs, bibliothèques en Europe entre les XIVe et XVIIIe siècles*. Paris: Alinéa, 1992.

[———. *The Order of Books: Readers, Authors, and Libraries in Europe Between the Fourteenth and Eighteenth Centuries*. Trans. Lydia Cochrane. Stanford: Stanford University Press, 1994.]

Clair, Jean. *Theimer: Notes pour un parcours*. Prague, 1996.

Commission Biblique Pontificale. *Bible et christologie*. Paris: Cerf, 1984.

Comte, Auguste. *Leçons de sociologie*. Intro. Juliette Grange. Paris: Flammarion, 1995.

Corcuff, Philippe. *Les nouvelles sociologies*. Paris: Nathan Université, 1995.

Dagognet, François. *Ecriture et iconographie*. Paris: Vrin, 1973.

———. *Eloge de l'objet*. Paris: Vrin, 1989.

———. *Rematérialiser, matières, et matérialisme*. Paris: Vrin, 1989.

———. *Le trouble*. Lyon: Les Empêcheurs de penser en rond, 1994.

Darnton, Robert. *Edition et sédition: L'univers de la littérature clandestine au XVIIIe*. Paris: Gallimard, 1991.

[———. *The Corpus of Clandestine Literature in France, 1769–1789*. New York: Norton, 1995.]

———. "La France, ton café fout le camp." *Actes de la recherche en sciences sociales*, no. 100 (December 1993).

Derrida, Jacques and Bernard Stiegler. *Echographies de la télévision*. Paris: Galilée, INA, 1996.

Dossier "Transmettre." *Catéchèse: Revue trimestrielle de pastorale* 1, no. 138 (1995).

Durkheim, Emile. *Les règles de la méthode sociologique*. Paris: Alcan, 1895.

———*The Rules of Sociological Method*. Trans. W. D. Halls. Ed. Steven Lukes. New York: Free, 1982.

Eisenstein, Elisabeth. *La révolution de l'imprimé dans l'Europe des premiers temps modernes*. Paris: La Découverte, 1991.

[———. *The Printing Press as an Agent of Change: Communications and Cultural Transformations in Early-Modern Europe*. 2 vols. New York: Cambridge University Press, 1979.]

L'Empire des techniques. Paris: Seuil, 1994.

Frodon, Jean-Michel. *L'âge moderne du cinéma français, de la Nouvelle Vague à nos jours*. Paris: Flammarion, 1995.

Gille, Bertrand. *Histoire des techniques*. Paris: Gallimard, Encyclopédie de la Pléiade, 1978.

Goguel, Maurice. *La foie à la résurrection de Jésus dans le christianisme primitif*. Paris: Ernest Leroux, 1933.

Goody, Jack. *Entre l'oralité et l'écriture*. Paris: Presses Universitaires de France, 1994.

[———. *The Interface Between the Written and the Oral*. Cambridge: Cambridge University Press, 1987.]

Gras, Alain. *Sociologie des ruptures*. Vendôme: Presses Universitaires de France, 1979.

Gras, Alain, Sophie Gras, and L. Poirot-Delpêche. *Grandeur et dépendance: Sociologie des macrosystèmes techniques*. Paris: Presses Universitaires de France, 1993.

Hagège, Claude. *Le souffle de la langue*. Paris: Odile Jacob, 1990.

Haskell, Francis. *Mécènes et peintres: L'art et la société au temps du baroque italien*. Paris: Gallimard, 1980.

[———. *Patrons and Painters: A Study in the Relations Between Italian Art and Society in the Age of the Baroque*. New Haven: Yale University Press, 1980.]

Heinich, Nathalie. *Ce que l'art fait à la sociologie*. Mimeograph. 1996.

———. *Du peintre à l'artiste: Artisans et académiciens à l'âge classique*. Paris: Minuit, 1993.

———. "La vidéo est-elle un art?" *Revue d'art et de sciences humaines*, no. 5 (1995).

Hennion, Antoine. "De l'étude des médias à l'analyse de la médiation: Esquisse d'une problématique." *Média-pouvoirs*, no. 20 (October–December 1990).

Hermès, no. 10. Directeur, Dominique Wolton. *Espaces publics, traditions, et communautés*. CNRS Editions, 1992.

Horkheimer, Max and Theodor W. Adorno. *La dialectique de la raison*. Paris: Gallimard, 1994.

[———. *Dialectic of Enlightenment*. Trans. John Cumming. New York: Continuum, 1987.]

Jacob, François. *Le jeu des possibles*. Paris: Livre de Poche, 1983.

———. *La logique du vivant: Une histoire de l'hérédité*. Paris: Gallimard, 1970.

[———. *The Logic of Life: A History of Heredity*. Trans. Betty E. Spillmann. New York: Pantheon, 1974.]

Jankélévitch, Sophie. "Durkheim: Du descriptif au nominatif." *Futur antérieur*, no. 5/6 (1993).

Johannot, Yvonne. *Tourner la page: Livres, rites, et symboles*. Grenoble: Jérôme Millon, 1988.

Kracauer, Siegfried. *Jacques Offenbach; ou, Le secret du Second Empire*. Paris: Le Promeneur, 1994.

[———. *Orpheus in Paris: Offenbach and the Paris of His Time*. Trans. Gwenda David and Eric Mosbacher. New York: Knopf, 1938.]

Laborde, Denis. *De Jean-Sébastien Bach à Glenn Gould: Magie des sons et spectacle de la passion*. Paris: L'Harmattan, 1997.

Lahire, Bernard. *La raison des plus faibles.: Rapport au travail, écritures domestiques, et lectures en milieux populaires*. Lille: Presses universitaires, 1994.

Landes, David. *L'heure qu'il est: Les horloges, la mesure du temps, et la formation du monde moderne*. Paris: Gallimard, 1987.

[Landes, David S. *Revolution in Time: Clocks and the Making of the Modern World*. Cambridge: Harvard University Press, 1983.]

Latour, Bruno. *Nous n'avons jamais été modernes: Essai d'anthropologie symétrique*. Paris: La Découverte, 1991.

[———. *We Have Never Been Modern*. Trans. Catherine Porter. Cambridge: Harvard University Press, 1993.]

——. *La science en action*. Paris: La Découverte, 1989.

[——. *Science in Action*. Cambridge: Harvard University Press, 1987.]

Le Moigne, Jean-Louis. *Le constructivism*. Vol. 1, *Des fondements*. Paris: Editions ESF, 1994.

Leroi-Gourhan, André. *Evolution et techniques*. Vol. 1, *L'homme et la matière*. Paris: Albin Michel, Sciences d'aujourd'hui, 1943.

——. *Evolution et techniques*. Vol. 2, *Milieu et techniques*. Paris: Albin Michel, Sciences d'aujourd'hui, 1945.

——. *Le geste et la parole*. Vol. 2, *La mémoire et les rythmes*. 1965. Reprint. Paris: Albin Michel, 1970.

——. *Le geste et la parole*. Vol. 1, *Technique et language*. 1964. Reprint, Paris: Albin Michel, 1974.

[——. *Gesture and Speech*. Trans. Anna Bostock Berger. Cambridge, Mass.: MIT Press, 1993.]

Lévy, Pierre. *Les technologies de l'intelligence: L'avenir de la pensée à l'ère informatique*. Paris: La Découverte, 1990.

Lévy, Pierre and Authier, Michel. *Les arbres de connaissances*. Pref., Michel Serres. Paris: La Découverte, 1992.

Mauss, Marcel. *Sociologie et anthropologie*. Paris: Presses Universitaires de France, 1950.

[——. *Sociology and Psychology: Essays*. Trans. Ben Brewster. London: Routledge and Kegen Paul, 1979.]

Melot, Michel, ed. *Nouvelles Alexandries: Les grands chantiers de bibliothèques dans le monde*. Paris: Cercle de Libraries, 1996.

Muglioni, Jacques. *Auguste Comte: Un philosophe pour notre temps*. Paris: Editions Kimé, 1995.

Offner, Jean-Marc and Denise Pumain, eds. *Réseaux et territoires: Significations croisées*. Paris: L'Aube, 1996.

Olender, Maurice, ed. "La transmission." *Le genre humain*, no. 3–4 (1982).

Parrochia, Daniel. *Philosophie des réseaux*. Paris: Presses Universitaires de France, 1993.

Péguy, Charles. *Note sur M. Bergson et la philosophie bergsonniene*. Oeuvres en prose, no. 3. Paris: Gallimard, 1992.

Perriault, Jacques. *La logique de l'usage: Essai sur les machines à communiquer*. Paris: Flammarion, 1989.

Piveteau, Jean-Luc. *Temps du territoire*. Geneva: Zoé, 1995.

Pottier, Bernard. *Les sciences du language en France au XXe siècle*. Paris: Société d'é-tudes linguistiques et anthropologiques de France, 1980.

Pseudo-Denys l'Aéropagite. *Oeuvres complètes*. Ed. M. de Gandillac. Paris: Aubier, 1943.

[Pseudo-Dionysius, the Areopagite. *The Divine Names and the Mystical Theology*. Trans. John D. Jones. Milwaukee: Marquette University Press, 1999.]

Rieusset-Lemarié, Isabelle. *Une fin de siècle épidémique*. Arles: Actes Sud, 1992.

Rilke, Rainer Maria. *Les elégies de Duino*. Paris: Paul Hartmann, 1936.

[———. *"Duino Elegies" and "The Sonnets to Orpheus."* Trans. A. Poulin, Jr. Boston: Houghton Mifflin, 1977.]

Roques, René. *L'univers dionysien: Structure hiérarchique du monde selon le pseudo-Denys*. Paris: Aubier, 1954.

Rosnay, Joël de. *L'homme symbiotique*. Paris: Seuil, 1995.

Rousseau, Jean-Jacques. *Discours sur l'origine de l'inégalité parmi les hommes*. Paris: Seuil, 1971.

[———. *Discourse on the Origin and Foundations of Inequality Among Men*. Trans. Roger D. Masters and Judith K. Masters. In Jean-Jacques Rousseau, *The First and Second Discourses*. Ed. Roger D. Masters. New York: St. Martin's, 1964.]

Ruffié, Jacques. *De la biologie à la culture*. Paris: Flammarion, 1976.

Sachot, Maurice. "Comment le christianisme est-il devenu 'religio.'" *Revue des sciences religieuses* 59, no. 2 (1985).

———. "Religio/Superstitio: Histoire d'une subversion et d'un retournement," *Revue de l'histoire de religions* 208, no. 4 (1991).

Séris, Jean-Pierre. *La technique*. Paris: Presses Universitaires de France, 1994.

Serres, Michel, ed. *Eléments d'histoire des sciences*. Paris: Bordas, 1989.

———. *Le tiers instruit*. Paris: François Bourin, 1991.

[———. *The Troubadour of Knowledge*. Trans. Shiela Faria Glaser and William Paulson. Ann Arbor: University of Michigan Press, 1997.]

Sève, Lucien. *Pour une critique de la raison bioéthique*. Paris: Odile Jacob, 1994.

Siegfried, André. *Itinéraires de contagions, épidémies, et idéologies*. Paris: Armand Colin, 1960.

Simmel, George. *La tragédie de la culture et autres essais*. Paris, Rivages, 1988.

[———. *Essays on Interpretation in Social Science*. Trans. Guy Oakes. Totowa, N.J.: Rowman and Littlefield, 1980.]

Simondon, Georges. *Du mode d'existence des objets techniques*. Paris: Aubier, 1958.

Sperber, Dan. *La contagion des idées*. Paris: Odile Jacob, 1996.

[———. *Explaining Culture: A Naturalistic Approach*. Oxford: Blackwell, 1996.]

Stiegler, Bernard. *La technique et le temps*. Vol. 1, *La faute d'Epiméthée*. Paris: Galilée, 1994.

[———. *Technics and Time*. Vol. 1, *The Fault of Epimetheus*. Trans. Richard Beardsworth and George Collins. Stanford: Stanford University Press, 1998.]

———. *La technique et le temps*. Vol. 2, *La désorientation*. Paris: Galilée, 1996.

Tarde, Gabriel. *Les lois de l'imitation*. Paris: Editions Kimé, 1993.

———. *L'opinion et la foule*. Paris: Presses Universitaires de France, 1989.

Tinland, Frank. *La différence anthropologique: Essai sur les rapports de la nature et de l'artifice*. Paris: Aubier, 1977.

Todd, Emmanuel. *La troisième planète: Structures familiales et systèmes idéologiques*. Paris: Seuil, 1983.

[———. *The Explanation of Ideology*. Trans. David Garrioch. Oxford: Blackwell, 1985.]
Vico, Giambattista. *La science nouvelle*. Paris: Gallimard, 1993.
[———. *The New Science of Giambattista Vico*. Rev. trans. of 3d ed. (1744). Trans. Thomas Goddard Hergin and Max Harold Fisch. New York: Cornell University Press, 1968.]

SUPPLEMENT TO ORIGINAL BIBLIOGRAPHY

Works by Régis Debray on Mediological Subjects

Contre Venise. Paris: Gallimard, 1995.
[*Against Venice*. Berkeley: North Atlantic Books, 1999]
Contretemps: Eloge des idéaux perdus. Paris: Gallimard, 1992.
Cours de médiologie générale. Paris: Gallimard, 1991.
Critique de la raison politique; ou, L'inconscient religieux. Paris: Gallimard, 1981.
[*Critique of Political Reason*. Trans. David Macey. London: Verso, 1983.]
A demain De Gaulle. Paris: Gallimard, 1990.
[*Charles de Gaulle: Futurist of the Nation*. Trans. J. Howe. London: Verso, 1994.]
L'état séducteur: Les révolutions médiologiques du pouvoir. Paris: Gallimard, 1993.
La France à l'Exposition universelle, Séville: Facettes d'une nation. Ed. Régis Debray. Pref. François Mitterand. Paris: Flammarion, 1992.
Manifestes médiologiques. Paris: Gallimard, 1994.
[*Media Manifestos: On the Technological Transmission of Cultural Forms*. Trans. Eric Rauth. London: Verso, 1996.]
L'oeil naïf. Paris: Seuil, 1994.
Le pouvoir intellectuel en France. Paris: Gallimard, 1979.
[*Teachers, Writers, Celebrities: The Intellectuals of Modern France*. Trans. David Macey. London: Verso, 1981.]
La puissance et les rêves. Paris: Gallimard, 1984.
Le scribe: Genèse du politique. Paris: Grasset, 1983.
Vie et mort de l'image: Une histoire du regard en Occident. Paris: Gallimard, Collection Folio/Essais, 1992.
Vie et mort de l'image. A film by Régis Debray and Pierre Desfons. Broadcast in the "Grand format" segment of *Arte*, Saturday, 14 October 1995, at 9:30 P.M.

Selected Essays by and Interviews with Régis Debray, in French and English

"A propos du spectacle: Réponse à un jeune chercheur." *Le Débat*, no. 85 (May–August 1995): 3–15.
"The Book as Symbolic Object." Trans. Eric Rauth. In *The Future of the Book*. Ed. Geoffrey Nunberg. Berkeley: University of California Press, 1996.
"Chemin faisant." *Le Débat*, no. 85 (May–August 1995): 53–61.

"A Few Remarks Apropos the 'Spectacle.' " In *Towards a Theory of the Image*, pp. 64–74. Ed. Jon Thompson. Maastricht: Jan van Eyck Academy, 1996.

"A Guerilla with a Difference." Trans. Elena Lledó. *NLR*, no. 218 (July/August 1996): 128–137.

"Histoire des quatre *M*" and "Paul Valéry." *Les Cahiers de médiologie*, no. 6 (2d semester 1998): 7–25.

"The Image vs. Language: Transmitting Symbols." Trans. Eric Rauth. *Common Knowledge* 4, no. 2 (fall 1995): 51–69.

"L'incomplétude: Logique du religieux?" *Bulletin de la société française de philosophie*, 90 (meeting of 27 January 1996): 1–35.

"The Myth of Art." *ViceVersa*, no. 49 (July–September 1995):30–34.

"A Plague Without Fleabites." Commentary in *Times Literary Supplement*, 4 July 1997, pp. 14–15.

"Pourquoi le spectacle?" *Les Cahiers de médiologie*, no. 1 (1st semester 1996): 5–13.

"Régis Debray Talks to Daniel Bougnoux." Interview in *UNESCO Courier*, February 1995, article 3, p. 5. (Available at http://web3.searchbank.com/infotrack.)

"Remarks on the Spectacle." Trans. Eric Rauth. *NLR*, no. 214 (November/December 1995): 134–141.

"Revolution in the Revolution." Interview with Andrew Joscelyne. *Wired* 3.01 (January 1995): 116, 161–162.

"The Small Screen Favors Caesar." Interview in *NPQ* 9, no. 2 (spring 1992): 35–41.

"La statue descellée par ses socles même." *Les Cahiers de médiologie*, no. 3 (1st semester 1997): 17–27.

"The Three Ages of Looking." *Critical Inquiry* 21 (spring 1995): 529–555. (Originally published as ch. 8 in Régis Debray, *Vie et mort de l'image: Une histoire du regard en Occident*. Paris: Gallimard, 1992, pp. 219–254.)

"Universal Art: The Desperate Religion." *NPQ* 9, no. 2 (spring 1992): 35–41.

Selected Critical Commentary on Debray and/or Mediology, in French and English

Anquetil, Gilles. "Quand un philosophe explore le monde des images." *Le Nouvel Observateur*, 12–18 November 1994, pp. 114–16.

Arénilla, Louis. "Un paysage d'idées" (on *Transmettre*). *La Quinzaine littéraire*, 16–30 April 1997, p. 20.

Billard, Pierre. "Images: Trajet d'une explosion." *Le Point*, 21 November 1992, pp. 31–32.

Biro, Yvette. "Creating Mediology: A Review of Régis Debray's *Vie et mort de l'image: Une histoire du regard en Occident.*" *Wide Angle: A Quarterly Journal of Film History, Theory, Criticism, and Practice* 18, no. 1 (January 1996): 69–73.

Cazeneuve, Jean. "Régis Debray: Haro sur l'image." *Le Figaro Littéraire*, 18 December 1992, p. 18.

Chartier, Roger, Dany-Robert Dufour, Roger Laufer, Jean-Louis Missika, and

Bernard Stiegler. "Identification d'un objet: La médiologie" (series of articles). *Le Débat*, no. 85 (May–August 1995): 3–61.

Clark, T. J. and Donald Nicholson-Smith. "Why Art Can't Kill the Situationist International." *October* 79 (winter 1997): 15–31.

Dauncey, Hugh. "More than a Charming Rhetorical Cloud" (on *Media Manifestos*). *Radical Philosophy* 83 (May/June 1997): 50–51.

Davey, Kevin. "In the Dock of Debray." Summary and interview in *New Statesman and Society* 7, no. 307 (17 June 1994): 20–22.

Droit, Roger-Paul. "Sous la culture, les luttes" [on *Transmettre*]. "La Chronique," *Le Monde*, 7 March 1997.

Dumas, Robert. "La médiologie: Un savoir nostalgique." *Critique*49, no. 552 (May 1993): 292–300.

Ferry, Luc and Alain Renaut. *French Philosophy of the Sixties: An Essay on Antihumanism*, pp. 42–48, 53, and 60–63. Trans. Mary H. S. Cattini. Amherst: University of Massachusetts Press, 1985.

Lövy, Michael. Review of *Transmettre*. *Archives de sciences sociales des religions*, no. 102 (winter 1998): 56–57.

Mulhern, Francis. "Introduction: Preliminaries and Two Contrasts." In Régis Debray, *Teachers, Writers, Celebrities: The Intellectuals of Modern France*, pp. vii–xxvi. Trans. David Macey. London: Verso, 1981.

Porter, Melinda. "Régis Debray," *Through Parisian Eyes: Reflections on Contemporary French Arts and Culture*, pp. 221–236. New York: Oxford University Press, 1986.

Reader, Keith. *Régis Debray: A Critical Introduction* Modern European Thinkers. London: Pluto, 1995.

Serres, Michel. "Hermès-Christ." *Le Nouvel Observateur*, 23 May 1991, pp. 29–30.

Spoiden, Stéphane. "Propos sur la médiologie: Entretien avec Régis Debray." *Contemporary French Civilization* 21, no. 2 (summer/fall 1997): 131–145.

INDEX

Louis Althusser	*Writings on Psychoanalysis: Freud and Lacan*
Elisabeth Roudinesco	*Jacques Lacan: His Life and Work*
Ross Guberman	*Julia Kristeva Interviews*
Kelly Oliver	*The Portable Kristeva*
Pierra Nora	*Realms of Memory: The Construction of the French Past* vol. 1: *Conflicts and Divisions* vol. 2: *Traditions* vol. 3: *Symbols*
Claudine Fabre-Vassas	*The Singular Beast: Jews, Christians, and the Pig*
Paul Ricoeur	*Critique and Conviction: Conversations with François Azouvi and Marc de Launay*
Theodor W. Adorno	*Critical Models: Interventions and Catchwords*
Alain Corbin	*Village Bells: Sound and Meaning in the Nineteenth-Century French Countryside*
Zygmunt Bauman	*Globalization: The Human Consequences*
Jean-Louis Flandrin and Massimo Montanari	*Food: A Culinary History*
Alain Finkielkraut	*In the Name of Humanity: Reflections on the Twentieth Century*
Julia Kristeva	*The Sense and Non-Sense of Revolt: The Powers and Limits of Psychoanalysis*

AEQ 7521